Managing
the
Unknowable

Ralph D. Stacey

Managing the Unknowable

STRATEGIC BOUNDARIES BETWEEN

ORDER

AND

CHAOS

IN

ORGANIZATIONS

Jossey-Bass Publishers · San Francisco

For sales outside the United States, contact Maxwell Macmillan International Publishing Group, 866 Third Avenue, New York, New York 10022.

Manufactured in the United States of America

The paper used in this book is acid-free and meets the State of California requirements for recycled paper (50 percent recycled waste, including 10 percent postconsumer waste), which are the strictest guidelines for recycled paper currently in use in the United States.

10% POST CONSUMER WASTE

Library of Congress Cataloging-in-Publication Data

Stacey, Ralph D.
  Managing the unknowable : strategic boundaries between order and chaos in organizations / Ralph D. Stacey — 1st ed.
    p.   cm.—(The Jossey-Bass management series)
  Includes bibliographical references and index.
  ISBN 1-55542-463-5
  1. Organizational effectiveness.   2. Strategic planning.
3. Management.   I. Title.   II. Series.
HD58.9.S737   1992
658.4—dc20   92-17306
                                                            CIP

FIRST EDITION
HB Printing   10 9 8 7 6 5 4 3 2 1   *Code 9262*

The Jossey-Bass
Management Series

**Consulting Editors
Organizations and Management**

Warren Bennis
University of Southern California

Richard O. Mason
Southern Methodist University

Ian I. Mitroff
University of Southern California

CONTENTS

PREFACE

It is by now clear to all that to survive the increasing onslaughts of international competition, organizations must be flexible and creative—that is, they must generate new strategic directions faster than their rivals. But most in the business community of the Western world have not yet come to realize that the way they generate strategic direction leaves them more likely to lag behind their competition than to surpass it. Let me explain why this is so.

Most Western managers believe that long-term success flows from a state of stability, harmony, predictability, discipline, and consensus—a state that I refer to as *stable equilibrium*. This belief leads them to demand general prescriptions that they can immediately convert into successful action. The most popular prescriptions are to formulate a vision of an organization's future state, to prepare long-term plans to realize that vision, to set strategic milestones and monitor achievements against those plans, to write mission statements and persuade people to share the same culture, to encourage widespread participation and consensus in decision making, and to install control systems that allow top executives to set the organization's direction and stay in command.

Few managers question the mind-set that leads to these prescriptions or the enthusiasm with which they are received. After all, this mind-set comes from our traditional scientific education and provides the basis for countless management textbooks and devel-

opment programs. The message is clear: managers either establish
stability and succeed or experience instability and fail.

But this fundamental mind-set, so regularly reinforced by
mainstream management literature, is simply wrong. And its consequences are significant: their intense preoccupation with stability
confines managers to strategies of repetition and imitation—they
either repeat their companies' past or imitate other organizations
that are moving on to better things.

If managers could relax their preoccupation with this mind-
set, with its use of stability as a defense against anxiety, they could
open up their potential for creativity. But in order to do this, managers must accept that the future direction of their organizations is
unknowable. This means that no one can have control of that future
direction; rather, the direction will emerge from the spontaneous,
self-organizing interaction between people. The process of letting
strategic direction emerge on its own is an exciting but unpredictable voyage of discovery—not a safe, predictable package tour.

In reality, success for an organization does not depend on
choosing stable equilibrium over explosive instability; it emerges
from a third condition that can be called *bounded instability*. Managers who intuitively understand this third state are not confined to
tired old patterns of repetition and imitation.

Why should this be so? Recent scientific discoveries have
shown that stable equilibrium is not a useful framework for understanding complex systems. These discoveries have revealed that the
continuous creativity found in natural systems is driven by stable
laws that generate specific kinds of instability within recognizable
patterns. Nature uses this bounded instability in a positive way to
generate variety and develop new directions. In nature, therefore,
success comprises both stability and instability.

Purpose of the Book

Managing the Unknowable will show that these new scientific insights also apply to business. In this book I explore what this new
understanding of bounded instability means, what difference it
makes to the actions managers must take to be successful, and what
consequences it holds for the way they approach the strategic man-

agement process. I will argue that Western managers need to embrace this new frame of reference, in which success is not stable equilibrium but a dynamic state of bounded instability that is far from equilibrium. When we focus on the world with this new mindset, we see that creativity is intimately connected with tension, conflict, and ever-changing perspectives.

The purpose of the book is to provoke managers into questioning their received wisdom about organizational control and considering the possibility of new strategic directions. The book presents a new mental model developed from scientific discoveries about complex systems. With that new mental model, managers will stop taking actions that waste time, lead to repetition and imitation instead of innovation, and provide excuses for ignoring the processes that really matter for strategic management. With the new model, managers will also be led to examine and improve the political interaction and group learning out of which new strategic directions emerge. The book uses discoveries about chaos and self-organization to provide a general framework that brings together a number of ideas that are beginning to influence managers—systems thinking, learning organizations, conflict management—and more traditional ideas of budgetary control and management by objectives.

Audience

The book will be of interest to all managers who would like their companies to have the creative edge that is necessary for businesses to succeed in the modern world. It will be particularly helpful to those who are trying to understand why certain companies in the Far East have been so phenomenally successful in recent years, and will provide a more realistic understanding of the role management plays in an unpredictable, often frightening business climate.

Overview of the Contents

Chapter One describes the current view that a successful business is one in stable equilibrium. The chapter then explains why this view is wrong and why a new mind-set is needed. The new view outlined in the chapter leads managers to face the fact that the long-term future of a business is unknowable and to realize that constant innovation, not stability, is the key to success in today's business environment.

Chapter Two describes the fast-moving business game and explains why formulating a vision and implementing plans will not enable a business to be a successful competitor in that game. It also presents recent powerful evidence that requires managers to question their current mind-set.

Chapter Three explains the scientific discoveries that have led to a new understanding of the state of chaos or bounded instability in nonlinear feedback systems. It also tells why a business can be viewed as such a system and what the implications of such a view are.

Chapter Four describes the seven steps undertaken by managers in successful businesses when they explore strategic issues within a chaotic framework. The chapter also suggests ways to handle strategic issues in a more creative fashion.

Chapter Five explores the question of whether the human mind can cope with chaos and, if so, how. It then explains how strategic thinking cannot be a step-by-step analytical process. Instead, it is provoked by anomaly and paradox and is an intuitive process that employs reasoning by analogy.

Chapter Six considers whether strategy formation can be intended ahead of time or whether it emerges from political interaction and learning. It is concerned with the role of prior, shared intention in the generation of strategic direction. It explains why the current preoccupation with "vision" and "common cultures" is harmful and describes what should replace these approaches.

Chapter Seven focuses on the topic of strategic control. It explains why a business's short term, which features situations of limited change, and its long term, which features situations of open-ended change, require completely opposite forms of control. The fact that both types of control must be used simultaneously produces a creative tension from which innovative strategies may emerge.

Chapter Eight discusses business structure. It explains why neither a completely rigid structure nor a highly flexible, "democratic" structure functions well when a business is developing new strategic direction. The role of empowerment in strategic management is explained.

Chapter Nine concludes the book by presenting seven steps that managers can follow to create the atmosphere in which new strategic direction can emerge. A featured part of these steps is the formation of self-organizing learning groups to explore strategic issues. These steps, however, are intended only as guides, not simple prescriptions, since there can be no simple prescriptions for the strategic management of an unknowable future.

Creative management lies in the reflective pause between a stimulus and the response to it. This book aims to provide a reflective pause for action-driven managers.

Acknowledgments

I would like to thank my colleagues Martha Birtles, John Mant, and Richard Turton for their comments and assistance. I am grateful to my M.B.A. students for their provocative questions and suggestions. Thanks to William Hicks, editor of the Jossey-Bass Management Series, and to Lisa Yount for an excellent editing job.

London, England Ralph D. Stacey
June 1992

—

THE AUTHOR

Ralph D. Stacey teaches strategic management at the Business School of the University of Hertfordshire in Hertford, England, and is a management consultant to top executive teams in a number of major companies. He received his B.Comm. degree (1963) from the University of the Witwatersrand in law and economics and his M.Sc. (1965) and Ph.D. (1967) degrees from the London School of Economics, both in economics.

Stacey's main research activities relate to processes of strategic management and organizational change. His publications include *The Chaos Frontier: Creative Strategic Control in Business* (1991) and *Dynamic Strategic Management for the 1990s* (1990).

From 1978 to 1984, Stacey was corporate planning manager of John Laing, Plc., one of the United Kingdom's top international construction companies. Prior to that he worked as an economist for John Laing and for the British Steel Corporation. He has also served as a financial investment strategist in the securities industry.

Managing
the
Unknowable

1

New Mind-Sets for Managing the Future

The aim of *Managing the Unknowable* is to change the way managers think about the route to business success. Today's dominant mind-set leads managers to think that they must find the right kind of map before they launch their businesses upon the perilous journey into the future. After all, the "common sense" belief is that you need to know where you are going and have some notion of how to get there before you set out on any journey.

Unfortunately, common sense often turns out to be a poor guide to successful action: the whole idea that a map can be drawn in advance of an innovative journey through turbulent times is a fantasy. This book will explain why it is impossible for managers to establish where they are going or how they are going to get there before they embark on a new business journey. Route and destination must be discovered through the journey itself if you wish to travel to new lands. The key to success lies in the creative activity of making new maps, not in the imitative following and refining of existing ones.

Old Maps: Routes to Stable Equilibrium

Most Western managers use the same fundamental navigational principles to find a route through the shoals of highly uncertain situations to the land of long-term business success. It is rare indeed for these principles to be questioned.

The first of these navigational principles is that an organization should have a visionary Chief Executive Officer (CEO) supported by a cohesive management team. Like the captain of a ship in troubled waters, a top executive is supposed to determine the future destination of an organization and guide it to that point. Effective top executives are in control of their organizations and their journeys because of their visions, the long-term plans they have devised, and the systems of rules and regulations they have installed. They tack and trim to keep the organization on course; when absolutely necessary they order a change in direction. The organizations go where they intend them to.

The second navigational principle is that an organization should have a common and unified culture. Managers and staff throughout a firm are supposed to share a single vision, believe in the same mission or business philosophy, and follow the same rules. They must "all pull together" and "sing off the same hymnsheet."

The third principle is that of focusing on "the bottom line." What will the rate of return be? What will the level of risk be? These are almost universally held to be the key questions to ask before taking any action.

The fourth principle is that a business should identify what it is good at and deliver what its customers want, doing so better than the competition. In other words, it must always stick to its core business, build on its strengths, and adapt more closely than its rivals to the market environment.

These four principles, when applied in a consistent and balanced manner, are supposed to lead a firm to success. Success, in this view, is quite clearly a state of stable equilibrium characterized by harmony, discipline, regularity, predictability, and adaptation. This is comforting because it suggests being "in control," avoiding surprises, knowing where you are going, reducing risks, and damping out differences. Belief that an organization is moving toward stable equilibrium reduces anxiety levels for everyone concerned.

The kind of behavior this mind-set leads to can be seen in just about every company in the United Kingdom and the United States. The following example is taken from an article on the Technology page of the *London Financial Times* for 19 December 1991. The article is headed "Shareholders Seek to Bring R&D Spending to Account." It reports on a move by the Institutional Shareholders Committee, supported by the Bank of England and the Department of Trade and Industry, to get companies to publish better information on their R&D efforts so that institutional shareholders can more actively exercise their rights and responsibilities as owners. The particular responsibility the Committee had uppermost in mind was that of pushing companies to spend more on R&D, thus increasing the rate of innovation. To achieve this, the Shareholders Committee demanded that companies (1) provide details on their overall strategy and the part R&D plays in it and (2) estimate likely rates of return and levels of risk on that expenditure.

The article goes on to explain that bodies such as the Electronics Equipment Association are resisting these demands. The only reason they give for doing so, however, is that fulfilling the demands would provide too much information to competitors. Nobody seems to have asked whether these proposals make sense in the first place, whether there is the remotest possibility that useful information of this kind could be provided, or whether all this control over levels of R&D expenditure actually leads to innovation.

The demands described in this article express a common concern with knowing what is going to happen, with being in control of innovation, and with the stability that all this implies. Behind this concern lies the assumption, unquestioned by everyone involved in the debate, that it is possible to know enough about what is going to happen to calculate meaningful future rates of return and levels of risk. Other unquestioned assumptions are that the process of innovation can be controlled from the top and that the bottom line should be preeminent. All taking part in this discussion are following an old map, a familiar route to stable equilibrium, in the comfortable conviction that it is right. But is it?

Making New Maps for Uncharted Waters

The trouble with standard maps and traditional navigational principles is that they can be used only to identify routes that others have traveled before: they can make sense only for managing the knowable. Only under familiar conditions can the captain identify the ship's future destination, and only under such conditions does it

make sense for the members of the team to follow the leader slav-
ishly. An old map is useless when the terrain is new. Old beliefs
cannot help in the task managers face today: managing the
unknowable.

   By definition, innovative strategic directions take an organization into uncharted waters. It follows that no one can know the
future destination of an innovative organization. Rather, that organization's managers must create, invent, and discover their destination as they go. If no one can know where the organization is
going, then no one can be "in control." Instead managers have to
create conditions in which behavior within the organization is controlled even though no one controls it. If managers cannot know
where the organization is going or what the right business philosophy for the future is, they should not all believe in the same things,
as the "cohesive team" and "common culture" myths hold. Instead,
they should question everything and generate new perspectives
through contention and conflict. Rather than building on their
strengths and merely adapting to existing market environments,
they must develop new strengths and at least partly create their own
environments. In general they must develop their navigational
principles, draw their maps, as they go along. To do this, they must
drop the old stable equilibrium mind-set and develop a new one
that recognizes the positive role of instability and the fact that long-
term futures are unknowable.

   An example of this kind of innovative journey can be found
in an article that sits right next to the one on R&D expenditure. The
headline of this article is "Sony Scattergun Hits the Target."

   The target in question is success for Sony's latest consumer
electronics product innovation, the Data Discman. The Discman is
a machine that sits easily in the palm of the hand. It can play
compact discs containing books, dictionaries, language lessons,
travel guides, quiz games, and other kinds of information. It includes pictures in a liquid crystal display as well as speech and
music. Before too long the Discman will enable people to carry a
reference library around in purse or pocket and call up passages
from many books within seconds.

   Sony is now churning out 20,000 of these personal information systems every month in Japan. In November 1991 it launched

the product in Germany and the United States. It will be launched in the United Kingdom, France, and Spain in the spring of 1992.

How did Sony develop this product? In 1988, a Sony employee, Yoshitaka Ukita, had to accept the failure of the 8 cm single compact disc player that he was responsible for developing: the machine was too late to secure a market against the competition. However, he did not just give up: he tried to think of an alternative use for the machine. He hit upon the idea of making it the heart of a personal information system. Ukita then built support among his colleagues for developing this idea further. They asked publishers to put reference material on compact discs and software writers to prepare the programs for organizing and retrieving data. They began to prepare a distribution system that encouraged both book stores and electronics stores to sell the product.

All this time the product was kept a secret even within Sony, partly to preserve the element of market surprise and keep the competition away, but also because the culture encouraged people to take an idea as far as possible on their own initiative. As the product launch date of 1 January 1990 approached, however, it became necessary to inform Norio Ohga, Sony's CEO. He backed the idea, making a design modification that improved the product even though it delayed its launch by six months. At first Sony expected to sell 5,000 units per month. Instead, they sold 8,000, and now they are producing 20,000 per month. Ukita expressed his surprise at this outcome. He and his colleagues agree that no one knows how the product will develop from here.

This example illustrates several important points. First, the top executives at Sony were not in control of developing the Discman, nor did they expect to be. Indeed they heard about it only when it was ready for launching. The immediate reaction of most Western managers is one of surprise at this failure to seek top management's prior approval for what turned out to be such an important project. Western managers recognize that individuals given greater freedom may be much more motivated to develop new ideas, but those managers cannot believe that an organization can be properly controlled if this kind of behavior is permitted. Nonetheless, the behavior of Ukita and his colleagues was controlled; it had a self-organizing quality.

Self-organizing control is a group phenomenon. It occurs when political interactions and dialogues between members of a group produce coherent behavior, despite the absence of formal hierarchy within that group or authority imposed from outside it. Informal groups and networks of managers within an organization clearly form and conduct themselves through self-organizing processes: no central authority organizes the network of informal contacts and coalitions that develop in an organization, and yet that network can behave in a controlled way and become a vital part of the organization's control system. Most managers are not used to the idea that a system, that is, a set of interactions, can control itself. For them, control requires some individual to take charge. The concept of self-organization, and the associated idea that systems can have a life of their own, are important ones in the new way of thinking about management developed in this book, ones we will be returning to a number of times, especially in Chapters Three, Four, and Seven.

Second, note that everyone involved in the Discman's development got their forecasts wrong. They simply had no idea whether the product would succeed or how well it might sell. They openly admit that they do not know what the future holds for the product now. They faced—and continue to face—the unknowable. The implications of our inability to say anything useful about the future of an innovative system, and thus for the possibility of envisioning and planning for that future, are discussed in Chapter Six.

Third, this new product is creating customer demand, rather than simply responding to existing needs. The creation process is one of trial and error that produces both success and failure. Sony's Walkman and camcorder are other prominent examples of its successes, while Betamax is a well-known example of its failure. These matters are discussed in Chapter Seven.

Finally, note how the Discman itself emerged from failure through trial and error, rather than being the realization of a vision or grand design. There was no map to follow before Ukita and his colleagues embarked on their journey: they made the map as they went along. The discussion in Chapters Five and Six deals with this point.

Examples such as the development of the Discman make it

clear just how absurd it is to ask companies to publish information on the rates of return and risk levels of their R&D expenditures. No one can possibly know these things if the R&D is going in anything like an innovative direction. Those who ask for this kind of information are insisting on old maps, whereas those who innovate are making new maps as they go.

Facing the Unknowable

Everyone admits that the future is basically unknowable, particularly in the case of an innovative product or course of action. This prospect, however, makes many managers uncomfortable, and they then ease their discomfort by assuming that even innovative futures are nonetheless approximately knowable. One can at least, they say, have a vision or make some assumptions about the long-term future. One can give shareholders, or others in a controlling position, meaningful information on future rates of return and risk levels.

I argue that this is a soothing fantasy that distracts attention from, and weakens the resolve to deal with, the real world. Instead of sidestepping the issue of unknowability, managers must learn to face it head on. That means accepting that you really have no idea what the long-term future holds for your organization; forming visions and making assumptions are not realistic possibilities. It means accepting that no individual or small group can be in control of an organization's long-term future and that securing uniformity by damping out differences between people is harmful. It also means sustaining contradictory positions and behavior within the same organization: Sony has budgets and hierarchies with power concentrated at the top, yet individuals and groups lower down in the hierarchy can pursue new ideas in relative freedom without having to keep justifying what they are doing to those much higher up. In the new way of thinking about management, a key concept is that of sustaining, rather than trying to resolve, this paradox of control and freedom.[1]

The new mind-set means positively using instability. Organizations that allow people to go far down the road of developing a product before involving top management (such as Sony) are bound to exhibit instability. Instead of regarding such instability as an unfortunate, unintended consequence of innovation, however, some Japanese companies purposely provoke it. For example, Honda hires large groups of midcareer managers from other organizations specifically to create alternative cultures. Honda thus encourages contention.

With the new mind-set presented in this book, a manager will use instability and crisis in a positive way to generate new perspectives and provoke the continual questioning and organizational learning through which unknowable futures are discovered and created. This new approach to management may be less comforting than the old one, but it is far more dynamic and far more useful in turbulent times. It is the approach required to lead managers away from the illusory goal of stable equilibrium and allow them to cope with the unknowable future of innovative organizations.

Coexistence of the Knowable and the Unknowable

Of course, everything is not unknowable. Most managers' jobs in fact are dominated by the knowable. Usually managers know what outcome they need to achieve in the short term and must merely solve the puzzle of how to do it. In other words, they know the destination but not the route. For this kind of normal puzzle-solving management, in which the basic framework is given and constant, it makes good sense to use quantitative analysis to identify solutions to problems and apply systematic, formalized types of planning, implementation, and control. Here the traditional mind-set is perfectly valid.

But at the same time, in the same organization, it is necessary to practice frame-breaking management, in which managers conflict, question, learn, and make new discoveries. This is the fundamental paradox of organization: the structures and behavior appropriate for normal stable management have to coexist with the informality and instability of the extraordinary form of management that is necessary to cope with the unknowable. This contradiction places great tension on successful organizations, but that tension can be the creative source of such organizations' continual development.

(**Stability and Cohesion: A Path to Early Death**)

We need a new approach to managing for two reasons. First, there is growing evidence that the old approach is not serving the world of business very well. This point, summarized in this section, is developed in Chapter Two. Second, the old approach is based on assumptions about the nature of systems that modern scientific discoveries are showing to be invalid. This matter is summarized in the next section and then explored in Chapter Three.

The fact that the current approach is not working well is shown in the relatively short lives of most organizations. In 1983, Shell conducted a survey of how long business organizations survive.[2] This survey revealed that corporations live about half as long as individual human beings. In other words your organization probably will die before you do! Bearing out this idea, a look at the Financial Times top 100 or the Fortune 500 over any recent five-year period will show how dramatically the listings change. And similarly, five years after Peters and Waterman had identified a sample of "excellent" companies,[3] two-thirds of these companies had slipped from the list. The simple truth is that we do not know how to sustain or replicate long life in organizations.

This rapid organizational turnover is unfortunate because resources are wasted and lives are disrupted every time an organization fails and a new one has to be set up. The learning process is also greatly slowed when firms so frequently have to go back to square one and start over.

It is becoming clearer why so many organizations die young. Recent studies increasingly make the point that managing by existing maps leads to imitation, repetition, and excess.[4] When they manage strictly within the mind-set that seeks stability, managers build only on their organization's existing strengths. They "stick to their knitting" and do better and better what they already do well. When some more imaginative competitors come along and change the rules of the game, such overadapted companies, like overspecialized animals faced with a major climate change, cannot respond fast enough. The former source of competitive success becomes the reason for failure, and the companies, like the animals, become extinct.

Texas Instruments provides an example.[5] It built its success on its ability to make certain products more cheaply and quickly than anyone else. At first it set the industry standards for semiconductors and produced an innovative flow of consumer products. Later, however, it became obsessed with cost reduction. TI offered its customers cheaper and cheaper, but shoddier and shoddier, products that were also outdated. The company was slow to move into more sophisticated chips, leaving these lucrative areas open to its rivals. In the end, TI was selling on the basis of price alone and ignoring the need to update its products. The source of TI's success became the reason for its decline because the company followed an old map, built on its strengths, and moved toward stable equilibrium. It found out the hard way that the successful, long-lived organization is not one that moves to stable equilibrium.

A New View of Organizational Dynamics

The second reason for dissatisfaction with today's dominant maps of business success is that those maps are based on highly questionable assumptions about the nature of organizational dynamics, that is, about the patterns of behavior generated by interaction between people in organizations. The current approach sees successful dynamics as intentional patterns of behavior that are regular and stable. This idea is valid only on the assumption that the behavior of an organization is predictable in principle. If it were not, it could hardly be intended or made regular and stable. Predictability and intention are possible only if there are direct, clear-cut connections between cause and effect—if a specific action in specific circumstances dependably leads to a specific outcome. Thus Federal Express is said to be a success because its founder, Fred Smith, had a vision of a new parcel delivery service and then set about realizing it. Honda is held to be a success because it carried out its founder's strategic intent to build motor engine competence. When we see a successful organizational effect, we look for the direct cause in some individual's vision. We believe quite firmly that order in a human system is intentionally put there by a designing mind.

If, however, it turned out that businesses were complex systems in which it was impossible to identify the specific ideas and actions that led to specific outcomes, then we would have to look for some other way of explaining the success of companies such as Federal Express and Honda. To advise managers to form visions in such circumstances would be to invite them to indulge in idle speculation, since they would be unable to identify the specific actions required to realize the vision. Only because we believe in direct cause-and-effect links does it make sense to talk about long-term goals and plans, visions, and missions. Only because we believe in the designing mind does it make sense to talk about redesigning whole organizations from scratch.

Systems analysts, however, have been telling us for years that in organizations the links between cause and effect can be complex, distant in time and space, and very difficult to detect.[6] These analysts have pointed to the unintended and counterintuitive results that complex organizations frequently produce. Few managers seem to have heard the message, however. Most continue to believe in straightforward connections between cause and effect, perhaps because it allows them to retain the comforting fantasy of "visions" and being "in control."

Mathematicians and natural scientists have recently made discoveries that make it much harder to continue to avoid facing up to the complex behavior of organizational systems. These scientists have shown that certain kinds of systems—they call them nonlinear feedback systems—operate in a state that they label "far from equilibrium." In this state, the system generates behavior that is unstable, but because it is unstable within limits that behavior is called bounded instability. This book will make it clear why an innovative business is just such a system and why its consequent bounded instability is a fact of immense importance to successful strategic management.

Basically, the dynamics of even simple nonlinear feedback systems are so complex that the links between cause and effect are lost in the detail of what happens. Tiny changes can escalate to have massive consequences; virtuous and vicious circles are generated. It is therefore totally impossible to predict the specific long-term future of such a system; that future is truly unknowable. The Discman example indicates that this conclusion has something to do with the world of business. At the end of 1987, when Ukita was developing the 8 cm compact disc player, neither he nor anyone else in the

world knew that his work would lead to Sony launching a successful new personal information system only two years later. The Discman resulted not from a single vision formulated at the top of the
organization but from a complex intertwining of events and people.
Ukita had no picture of a future state—even now he admits that he
does not know what the future holds for his product. Instead, he was
driven by a challenge arising in the present. How that challenge led
to a new product depended upon his interaction with others.

But while specific behavior is unpredictable when a system
is far from equilibrium, that unpredictable behavior falls within the
boundaries of recognizable categories. These are qualitative similarities, "family resemblances," and constant irregularities that skilled
people can recognize and cope with through intuition and reasoning by analogy. The inspiration for developing the personal information system came to Ukita when he juxtaposed the failed 8 cm
CD player with a Filofax and an electronic personal organizer. His
reasoning by analogy no doubt was also influenced by the successful
Walkman, or personal entertainment system. Ukita and his colleagues had learned from the Betamax failure as well. There, weak
links with film distributors had been one of the undoings of the
product. To avoid a similar problem, Ukita and his colleagues
made sure that they formed links with publishers and bookstores.

Overall, then, the dynamics of nonlinear feedback systems
are characterized by a combination of regularity and irregularity, of
stability and instability. Systems of this kind develop over time by
passing through periods of instability, crisis, or chaos and then
spontaneously making choices at critical points, producing new
directions and new forms of order.[7] Scientists are now thinking
about systems in nature as having lives of their own, communicating, making choices, and creating new forms of behavior. These
ideas will be clarified in Chapter Three.

This book contends that all business organizations are nonlinear feedback systems. Such systems fail—they simply repeat their
past history—when they are taken to positions of stable equilibrium. They succeed—that is, they are innovative or creative—when
they are sustained far from equilibrium in states of bounded instability.[8] The central message of the "new science" for business people is this: organizations are feedback systems generating such

complex behavior that cause-and-effect links are broken. Therefore, no individual can intend the future of that system or control its journey to that future. Instead, what happens to an organization is created by and emerges from the self-organizing interaction between its people. Top managers cannot control this, but through their interventions they powerfully influence it. It is their prime responsibility to understand the qualitative patterns of behavior that their interventions may produce. Order through installation by the designing mind is replaced by order emerging from instability through a process of self-organization.

Managing the Dynamic Organization

If they adopt the new mind-set suggested by these findings about system dynamics, managers will see the world of organizations in a very different way. Instead of following the old navigational principles described at the beginning of this chapter, which lead toward the goal of stability, they will design their actions according to the following propositions of a dynamic far-from-equilibrium model of organizing:

- The long-term future of an innovative organization is unknowable: it cannot be predicted to any useful extent. This follows from what scientists have discovered about nonlinear feedback systems, of which a business organization is one. The unpredictability arises from the very structure of the business system, not simply from changes in markets and technology.
- If the future is inherently unpredictable, it follows that a single, organization-wide "shared vision" of a future state must be impossible to formulate, unless we believe in mystic insight. Any such vision that managers put forward is then bound to be either a dangerous illusion or an interpretation of what has happened made with the benefit of hindsight. The same point must apply to long-term plans designed to realize such visions. If we have to use the word "vision," we will have to be careful that we understand it to be one of many current challenges and aspirations being pursued by individuals. (This question of the role of visions, backed by examples, is discussed in Chapter Six.)

- Instead of visions and plans, effective managers focus on ever-changing agendas of strategic issues, challenges, and aspirations. These arise out of poorly structured and conflicting changes that occur in the present but have long-term, widespread consequences. Such a rapidly changing agenda means that the organization does not hitch its future to any one development; only with hindsight can a "vision" or "grand design" be detected. Think how well this describes the continuing agenda of product developments, failures, and successes at Sony.
- A unified, strongly shared culture blocks an organization's ability to develop and handle changing strategic agendas. For example, the bureaucracy and unified culture of General Motors has led it to follow for decades the same strategy of covering the whole market with a standard product line. By contrast, Honda promotes multiple, contradictory cultures to foster different perspectives and provoke the questioning and complex learning that are necessary to handle changing strategic agendas.[9]
- Cohesive teams of managers—working in the hierarchy of bureaucracy—operating in consensus are required for day-to-day, problem-solving management. However, learning groups of managers—working in spontaneously self-organizing networks—that encourage open conflict, engage in dialogue, and publicly test assertions are vital to the handling of strategic issues.
- The hierarchy/bureaucracy exists to preserve and ensure the efficient operation of the status quo. The self-organizing political network of contacts between people functions to undermine and destroy that hierarchy/bureaucracy. Without this paradox and the consequent tension between control and freedom there could be no change.
- Normal, day-to-day management must rely on decision making through a logical, analytical process. But the extraordinary management required to uncover strategic issues and handle them in innovative ways has to rely on decision making that results from an exploratory, experimental process based on intuition and reasoning by analogy.
- Normal, day-to-day control and development of a business requires comparison of progress against plan milestones and the

taking of corrective action. This kind of control means constraint by rules, systems, and rational argument. But the control and development of a business in the open-ended, unknowable long term is a political process in which the constraints are provided by the need to build and sustain support. It is also a learning process in which constraint is provided by dialogue and the need to persuade through argument. Political interaction and learning activity in a sophisticated group of people is a self-policing form of control. The group interaction itself produces the control. Ukita would never have gotten anywhere with his Discman idea if he had failed to build support from his colleagues and ultimately obtain the backing of Sony's chief executive. That was a political process. Similarly, while the Discman was being developed, there was no measuring against preestablished milestones. But this did not mean that Ukita and his colleagues were out of control. Rather, the constraint was provided by the political interaction and dialogue between themselves.

- New strategic directions emerge spontaneously from the chaos of challenge and contradiction, through a process of real-time learning and political interaction. The Shareholders Committee's proposed rules on R&D expenditure disclosure were wrong because they did not take such spontaneity into account. Trying to impose rules like this is a static approach that can work only for normal management, not for the frame-breaking management that R&D should involve.

- Top executives do not drive and control new strategic directions. Instead, effective top executives create favorable conditions for, and participate in, complex learning and effective politics.

- Normal, day-to-day management can be guided by general models and traditional prescriptions that apply to many different specific situations. Comprehensive systems and programs can be installed to achieve this. Innovation and new strategic directions, however, require the development of new mental models—new maps—for each new situation. In other words, no person, no book, can prescribe systems, rules, policies, or methods that dependably will lead to success in innovative organizations. All managers can do is establish the conditions that enable groups of people to learn in each new situation what approaches are effective in handling it. There cannot be comprehensive installation, only piecemeal intervention at sensitive points in the system.

• Continuing success flows from creative interaction with the market environment, not simply from building on existing strengths. Sony does the former with its Walkmans, camcorders, and Discmans. Texas Instruments spent years in the 1980s doing the latter with its mania for cost cutting. Building on existing strengths seeks equilibrium at the cost of success; innovation creates success through intentionally steering away from equilibrium.

A Word of Clarification

There are always at least a few people at management seminars, or in book reviews, who draw the following conclusion from what has just been set out: "You are telling us that there is no point in bothering with the long-term future because it is unknowable. All we have to do, then, is manage the short term as tightly as possible and be ready to react flexibly to whatever else happens. Basically there is little we can do except reduce our risk exposure and let the long term take care of itself."

This kind of response means that the person making it is looking at the world through the lenses of the old stable-equilibrium mind-set. From that perspective, abandoning visions and long-term plans means abandoning all concern with the long term. This is most emphatically not the message of this book. The dynamic far-from-equilibrium model of strategic management involves handling present issues that have widespread long-term consequences in a more innovative and more creative way, not abandoning such issues. That more creative way is a process of real-time, complex learning, not the static linear activity of long-term planning.

Most of us immediately think of adult learning as the independent activity of an individual performed during time especially set aside for that purpose. According to this view, we learn when we take time off from our main activities to attend lectures, read textbooks, or analyze problems. Once we have learned the lesson, we return to our regular activities and apply it. This is rather like preparing and loading the data input for a computer program and then running the program. In the terminology of the computer scientists this is not "on line" or in "real time."

The formulation of visions and the preparation of long-term plans well in advance of action is just this kind of learning. For example, managers go away for a weekend to a country retreat in order to develop a mission statement and prepare a plan; then they return to the office on Monday morning to begin the real work of carrying these out. They learn out of real time and they apply that learning as they act in real time.

In fact, of course, we learn all the time—and this day-to-day learning is far more important than anything that emerges from a book or seminar. We learn every day at the workplace in groups as those groups act to deal with the problems and opportunities of the business. This is what the computer scientist would describe as "on line" or in "real time" because the learning and the doing proceed hand in hand, immediately affecting and interacting with each other. The most important learning we do flows from that trial-and-error action we take in real time and especially from the way we reflect on those actions as we take them. When we face the unknowable we cannot set aside time to learn out of real time because, by definition, we do not know what we are supposed to learn. We can only learn "on the hoof."

How well people learn under these circumstances depends on how they interact with each other in groups—that is, on group dynamics. For example, an executive team may be driven by the dynamics of fight or flight. They alternate between fierce internal rivalry concerning strategic issues and avoidance of those same issues in order to prevent the conflict that those issues arouse. A team driven by such dynamics cannot deal effectively with strategic issues, no matter how intellectually sound their individual analyses may be, because their dynamics get in the way of their joint learning.

Another team, driven by the dynamics of dependence on a single charismatic leader, will never learn much either because they will never offer new ideas. They will simply follow the leader, whether to success or over a cliff. It follows that the strategic choices an executive team makes depend far more on the nature of the dynamics in their group than on any rational consideration. Those dynamics in turn depend upon how people use power, how they exert authority, and how they fill their roles.

So, when this book claims that visions and long-term plans are merely fantasy defenses against anxiety, it is not recommending that you shut your eyes to the long term. On the contrary, it invites you to drop the fantasy defense and open your eyes to the only processes that are realistically available for dealing with the unknowable long term: the processes of real-time learning in groups, of reasoning by analogy, and of relying on intuition. It directs your attention away from imaginary obstacles such as lack of information, techniques, or prescriptions and toward the real obstacles, which have to do with the way power is used and the impact this has on group dynamics and the effectiveness of your organization's political system.

Furthermore, when you see the world through the new lenses, you will realize that you cannot reduce your risk by simply letting the long term take care of itself. Common sense may tell you that doing nothing or doing only what seems absolutely safe is the best way of dealing with unknowable futures. Yet again, however, common sense turns out to be a poor guide. For, in complex systems, even doing nothing could have escalating consequences as could some chance aspect of something that seems to be absolutely safe. You may as well, then, take a chance and do something positive, even though you cannot know its outcome and it too could fail. If the consequences of doing something and doing nothing are both unknowable, how can you know which is safer? Instead of trying to reduce your risk, you will be more inclined to take risks and be creative when you really face up to the unknowability of the long-term future.

The old mentality encourages you to do nothing, or merely more of the same, until you know what will happen—until you can calculate the rate of return and specify the risk level. It makes it sound reasonable to do only enough to earn an acceptable rate of return. But the new mentality makes it clear that there is no point in waiting until you know what will happen since you never can.

You cannot eliminate the risk and stay in business. You have to take a chance and keep learning.

Another response to the new mental model is to say that all these informal group learning and political processes are no good for large, complex organizations, which require tight, formal systems. Again this response reveals the power of the old mind-set. When you look at the world of organizing through the new lenses, you do not see "either/or" choices. Instead, you see "both/and" choices. Successful organizations—that is, continually innovative organizations—cannot choose between tight, formal control systems and structures on the one hand and loose, informal processes that provoke learning on the other. Whether they are large or small, successful organizations must have both at the same time. This is because they must all simultaneously handle both the knowable, closed changes involved in the day-to-day running of the existing business and the unknowable, open-ended changes involved in the innovative development of the business. The result is certainly organizational tension, paradox, and never-ending contradiction, but this provokes conflict and learning and thus is the source of creativity.

From Order to Disorder: Changing the Frame of Reference

The most daunting task facing managers today lies at a far deeper and more disturbing level than the obvious one of coping with turbulent change. Most managers, preoccupied with stability and obvious forms of control, are not taking sufficient account of the dynamics of long-term business success. The real challenge, therefore, is to develop a more appropriate frame of reference through which to understand the unstable dynamics of business organizations and to design creative actions. It is the mental models that managers employ, not some bag of tools or techniques, that determine their ability to deal with the unknowable. This book is therefore concerned with mental models—with different ways of thinking —rather than with specific prescriptions or tactical recommendations. Managers with robust mental models make up their own prescriptions as they go along.

It is the aim of this book to encourage managers, consultants, and researchers to question today's dominant model of the successful business, that of an organization in stable equilibrium. This book will develop the proposition that because we fail to think explicitly of a successful business as a dynamic feedback system generating complex, unstable behavior, we also fail to identify the actions needed for continuing success.

The next chapter describes in more detail the reasons for concluding that today's dominant frame of reference for understanding business is inadequate and for insisting that a new mindset is needed. The chapters following explore how this new mindset helps to answer the key questions managers today ask about their task:

- What kind of organization do we need if we are to be successful in today's obviously unstable conditions?
- What do we need to do to generate continuing creativity and innovation in our business?
- What is strategic thinking, and how do we do it in irregular and contentious circumstances?
- How do we establish strategic direction and intention when the future is unknowable?
- How do we control our business strategically when the future is open-ended and unpredictable?
- How do we secure participation and unleash the creative potential of the people in our business?

In everyday business life, managers must answer questions like these while surrounded by a world that is quite clearly characterized at the same time by stability and instability, predictability and unpredictability, regularity and irregularity, contention and consensus, intention and chance. The world they face is a paradox: intertwined order and disorder. Yet when they try to explain what is going on and design actions flowing from those explanations, they almost always approach the task from the perspective of order and largely ignore the role of disorder. This book will turn that perspective on its head, looking at the business world from the angle of disorder to see how it is intertwined with order.

The reader no doubt has heard the following joke: One night

a woman is walking down a dark street. She comes to a pool of light under a streetlamp and sees a man on his knees there, obviously looking for something. She asks, "What are you looking for?"

"A coin I have lost," the man replies.

"Well, where did you lose it?" the woman inquires.

"Over there," he responds, pointing to a dark area between two streetlights.

"Why on earth are you looking here, then?" comes her puzzled question.

"Because the light is better here," is his exasperated reply.

This old joke encapsulates the message of this book. Today most of us are trying to explain a messy, opportunistic global competition game using mental models that focus on order, stability, cohesion, consistency, and equilibrium. We are not paying enough attention to the irregular, disorderly, chance nature of the game. We do this because it is easier and more comfortable than feeling about in the dark for explanations that describe the world in terms of disorder, irregularity, unpredictability, and chance. This book is concerned with the insights—the illuminations if you will—that those darker explanations have to give.

2

The Failure of Conventional Management: Using Orderly Strategies in a Disorderly World

When managers design actions to control and develop their business, most do so within a commonly accepted mental framework. They believe unquestioningly that businesses achieve success when they are controlled from the top and plan to realize some overarching shared vision of the future. Success in this view is defined as purposeful movement toward stable equilibrium. This chapter develops the reasons why practical managers now need to question their exclusive focus on stability, regularity, predictability, and cohesion. Such a focus is bound to produce inadequate responses to the dynamic competition game that managers must play if their organization is to survive.

The Dynamic Competition Game

Eastman Kodak has been selling photographic materials in Japan since the late nineteenth century. After World War II, however, it scaled down its operations in what was then a relatively unimportant market. It handed over the marketing of its products to Japanese distributors for political reasons. These seemingly unimportant actions taken long ago had consequences that accumulated slowly to have impacts on geographically distant markets. Specifically, they contributed to the ability of Fuji to build up a 70 percent share of the Japanese market, leaving Kodak with less than 10 percent of that market by the beginning of the 1980s. Once it had established a secure position in its home market, Fuji turned its attention to the American and European markets, where Kodak enjoyed a lucrative dominance in color film. Throughout the 1980s Kodak suffered the onslaughts of Fuji, which forced it into panic cost-cutting exercises that were not always successful. The Kodak share price underperformed for years, prompting rumors of eventual breakup.

In 1984 Kodak began to strike back. It invested $500 million to build up a Japanese operation. It regained control of distribution in this market, encouraged locals to invest in the equity of the Japanese subsidiary, and spent heavily on advertising and promotion. The result was a sixfold sales increase, giving Kodak a 15 percent share of the Japanese market. The operation is only now making a profit, and it will take years to pay back the original investment. Nonetheless, Kodak's retaliation squeezed Fuji's margins in its home market and put it on the defensive in the American and European markets as well. Fuji was forced to divert resources from overseas in order to defend itself at home.

One trivial but amusing example of the Kodak-Fuji "war" involved airships. Kodak spent $1 million on an airship sporting its logo, which it floated over Fuji's Tokyo head office. Articles in Japanese newspapers poking fun at Fuji resulted. Fuji then had to spend much more than Kodak to bring its own airship from Europe for a face-saving promotion in Tokyo.[1] Even this small incident demonstrates the interactive feedback nature of the worldwide competitive game: relatively small actions in one place can feed back into actions and consequences in another, in a self-reinforcing manner.

The same point is illustrated by the consumer electronics industry—where the victory went to the Japanese. During the late 1960s and early 1970s, Japanese companies detected "loose bricks" in the black-and-white and small-screen television set markets in America and Europe. They soon dominated these relatively unattractive segments of the overall television set market. They used their positions and cash flows there to mount attacks on many other consumer electronics markets.

These stories demonstrate the most obvious problem facing managers today: how to make and enact strategic choices in a highly interconnected and fiercely competitive world. To survive in even the most powerful international companies, managers must continually preempt, counter, ward off, and initiate creative competitive moves to attract and retain customers. They must play a fast-moving interactive game, increasingly on a global scale, in which playing conditions and rules both change rapidly. The pace of the game has been speeding up and will continue to do so.

The players in this worldwide game frequently get caught up in self-reinforcing vicious and virtuous circles. A company that starts to lose out in one market soon will lose out in others. Conversely, one may gain a foothold, then use a chink or a crack in a market to build small positions that lead to self-reinforcing virtuous circles, as the Japanese did in the television set market.

The game is the same whether it is played in a global or a local setting. It is an unstable game, full of surprises, with outcomes that cannot be predicted. Success goes to the nimble, the creative, the innovative players who design their moves with an understanding of the dynamics of the game. The winners are those who understand the sometimes gradually accumulating, sometimes rapidly escalating patterns of competitive interaction that take place both geographically and over time and who choose their actions accordingly.

Managers, consultants, and researchers are all perfectly aware of this and often unconsciously use this knowledge as they play the game. When managers in North America and the United Kingdom formally sit down to design their game strategy, however, they act as if they had never heard of these essential characteristics of the game.

Static Responses: Visions and Plans

I recently facilitated a series of workshops with a group of top managers in a company facing a market that was becoming much more competitive than it had been before. The purpose of the workshops was to review how those managers were handling the new challenges. They proved to be approaching them in much the same way as most of the competent managers I had worked with in other companies. They began by trying to find out what their customers thought of them and what those customers now wanted from them. Through market research, they discovered that their major group of customers regarded them as distant, unresponsive, and inefficient. According to the research, the customers wanted a company that was innovative in dealing with issues of environmental protection, customer care, and efficiency. They were looking for an assertive, dynamic, proactive company that would work in partnership with them. How were these customer requirements to be met?

The consultants who carried out this research recommended that the company adopt a corporate vision of their company as "The Innovators" in their industry. This vision, they said, would provide future direction and act as a framework or blueprint for focused, consistent, and cohesive management decision making. It also would provide a motivating purpose for employees and a strategy for communicating with customers, suppliers, shareholders, and the media. Within this guiding framework, units of the business would differentiate themselves and their products through improved customer care and efficiency. The vision would also differentiate the company from its competitors and add value to its products and services. In short, the purpose of the vision was to create stability both within the company and externally.

The company turned to other consultants for advice on how to implement this vision. They were told to set up a systematic planning and development process to deliver a strategy of growth within the overall vision. First, the consultants said, the company should prepare three levels of plans: a corporate plan, business unit plans, and product plans. Then they should set about implementing those plans.

In short, the consultants recommended that all actions be centrally controlled and guided by a shared overall intention to which everyone in the organization was committed. Their emphasis was quite clearly on order, stability, consistency, and harmony. They stressed the use of analytical techniques, step-by-step thinking, top-down control, and long-range planning.

At the meeting during which these proposals were discussed, some of the company's managers expressed limited skepticism, but no one rejected the consultants' advice outright. Over the past few years I have seen similar proposals treated in much the same way, over and over again. They represent a received wisdom that is widely, if sometimes uneasily, accepted by both managers and the consultants they look to for advice. That received wisdom is also firmly embedded in the textbooks on management and organization.

Recommendations to play the competitive game in an orderly, consistent manner, however, sit rather oddly with the description of that game given earlier as fast moving, messy, characterized by escalation and self-reinforcing circles, full of surprises and unpredictable outcomes. The game is dynamic, interactive, and nonlinear, moving in circles with cause and effect distant from each other. How, then, can a static approach based on straight-line thinking with close links between intention and outcome succeed in it? There is now impressive evidence that it cannot.

Lack of Evidence Linking Plans to Success

Many of those committed to long-term planning recognize the mismatch between their prescriptions and the dynamic competition game, but they claim that the process has benefits even if the outcome is not directly useful. The benefits claimed are help in defining strategic problems and bringing about an orderly approach to those problems; generation of useful information; revelation of decision makers' value judgments; and general assistance in making strategic choices.[2] If this were true, we would expect to find some connection between strategic planning systems and superior performance.

However, when companies that utilize a strategic planning approach are compared with those that do not, no reliable evidence that the former perform better has been found. Greenley recently surveyed nine studies that had looked for a statistical connection between strategic planning and performance in manufacturing companies.[3] Eight of these studies were carried out in the United States and one in the United Kingdom. Sample sizes varied from 10 to 386 companies. Five studies concluded that there is a connection between strategic planning and performance, but the other four failed to find convincing evidence of such a connection. Of the two studies with the fewest methodological deficiencies, one found a connection between planning and performance and the other found none. And even these two studies, both of which applied to the

United States, can be criticized on logical grounds. Other factors besides planning affect performance, and these cloud the connection—or lack of it—between planning and performance. It thus is not at all clear from statistical tests whether planning leads to good performance. We have to rely instead on anecdotal evidence.

Many anecdotal studies do report close links between managers with visions, perhaps supported by long-term plans, and successful organizations. I will argue in Chapter Six, however, that the link that researchers keep finding between success and vision as a picture of a future state is simply a reflection of the stable equilibrium mind-set with which those researchers approach their task. I will also argue that much of this evidence is concerned with visions that are something other than a picture of a future state. Researchers frequently use the label "vision" to describe what would more appropriately be called a challenge or an aspiration, that is, a driving force that arises in the present and requires no knowledge of the future. Alternatively, researchers categorize as "vision" the values and business philosophies that have emerged from the past; these also require no knowledge of the future. Challenge, aspiration, and business philosophy are all essential contributors to success, but there is little reliable evidence that this conclusion also applies to some kind of picture of the future or a comprehensive plan for making that picture come true.

There is therefore no reliable evidence that visions of the future and plans lead to improved performance. There are, however, a number of pieces of research that, taken together, provide powerful reasons for a fundamental reexamination of vision/plan prescriptions.

Why Plans Are Not Used for Strategic Control

In a recent study of the top 250 companies in the United Kingdom, only 11 percent of the sample replying to a questionnaire said that they set long-term milestones and then monitored performance against them. In-depth interviews with a number of companies in the sample revealed that even fewer monitored their strategic plans in a formal way. Those that did monitor their plans formally used events (such as building a new factory) rather than results-based milestones.[4]

For at least thirty years now, managers have been strongly advised to prepare and use long-term plans as a central part of their strategic control system. Most say that they agree with this advice, but the research evidence shows quite clearly that when they act, they do not really follow that advice. They may prepare long-term plans, but because they fail to monitor them, the prescribed strategic control system is absent.

The authors of the study ascribe this failure to "short term-ism." They claim that "short termism," in turn, is due to the manner in which the financial markets operate. Companies in America and the United Kingdom, they point out, depend primarily upon equity capital for their financing. The major providers of this capital are institutional fund managers, whose performance is measured against very short-term (quarterly) share price criteria. These managers consequently demand high short-term profit levels. Managers in industry and commerce thus have no option but to take a short-term view if they are to avoid undervalued shares and attendant takeover risks. Consequently, such managers avoid taking actions that have long payback periods or high levels of risk. Financial market pressures therefore compel managers to avoid innovative long-term behavior. The authors of the study claim that this is why most companies have short-term planning or budgetary systems but fail to use long-term planning effectively. They also say this is why most managers do not appraise capital projects using rational discounted cash flow techniques.[5]

Although this argument is widely disseminated in the media, frequently put forward by academics, and supported by many managers themselves (perhaps because it puts most of the blame on the financial institutions), there does not seem to be very strong evidence to support it. First, there is not much evidence that fund managers actually behave in a manner conditioned entirely by the next three months. After all, they expect their careers to last far longer than that. If they build portfolios of shares in companies that simply make a fast profit, they may achieve good performance for a short while, but the whole portfolio could well collapse after that. Secondly, studies have shown that share prices rise when companies announce major investment or R&D programs.[6] Thus it appears to be something of a myth that stock markets force managers to focus strictly on the short term.

The studies that debunk this myth tend to put the blame for "short termism" on the managers of industrial and commercial companies instead. Their argument is that "short termism" is the consequence of reward structures tied to short-term profit performance, lack of effective control based on long-term planning, and widespread use of payback investment appraisal techniques that have a bias toward the short term. The implication is that if managers had different reward structures, they would adopt forms of control that involved longer-term planning and would appraise investments using discounted cash flow techniques. All would then be well.

Still other critics lay the blame for ineffective long-term planning at the door of internal politics. These critics say that managers make decisions that will advance their own careers, even if those decisions are not in the company's best interests. By trying to build departmental and business unit empires, managers obstruct the formulation and implementation of sensible long-term plans and the achievement of visions.

In short, when observers see that managers do not use long-term plans effectively, they tend to claim this happens because financial markets and reward systems discourage long-term planning or because managers play selfish politics. This reasoning leads to prescriptions for renewed efforts to remove these obstacles and use long-term plans as part of an effective strategic control system. But is this the right response? Do managers really fail to use these rational techniques, after decades of agreeing with the advice to do so, because they are at the mercy of the financial markets or are incredibly short-sighted and selfish? Or are managers not using the prescriptions for strategic control because the whole idea is completely inappropriate? This book will argue that managers do not use the proposed strategic control system because it is impossible to do so.

Changes Needed in Current Thinking
on Strategic Management

Even when managers do not follow vision/plan prescriptions, the framework underlying these prescriptions continues to have a heavy influence on these managers' strategic thinking. A number of important studies have recently concluded that the quality of strategic thinking that results is a significant cause of declining Western competitiveness. The implication is that this framework, the stable equilibrium mind-set, needs to be changed.

When managers think of strategic management as a process of realizing visions through actions planned a long time in advance, they by definition focus their attention on securing a widely shared commitment to achieve a foreseeable future state. They try to design a pattern in actions that is cohesive, consistent, and integrated. They try to produce regularity and to sustain stable equilibrium, both internally and externally.

In practice, however, actions and their consequences can be regular and foreseeable only when they represent repetitions of the past; that is, repetitions of what managers have done and are already doing well. The vision/plan mentality therefore leads managers to design courses of action that reinforce the direction already established for their business. Such managers build on their company's strengths, stick to their core businesses, and make only small, logically incremental changes. When managers focus on the predictable, their actions too become predictable. They will be successful while their world remains stable, but when their rivals change that world too much, they will fail. A number of studies spell out the harmful consequences of this behavior pattern.

Creating Rather than Adapting

In an article in the *Harvard Business Review*, Hamel and Prahalad report on their study of a number of international companies.[7] They suggest that the noticeably successful (Honda, Komatsu, and Canon, for example) can be distinguished from the noticeably less so (General Motors, Caterpillar, and Xerox, for example) by the different mental models of strategy that guide their respective managers' actions.

Managers in the successful companies, according to Hamel and Prahalad, are driven by strategic intent; that is, a challenging shared vision of a future leadership position for their company that is stable over time. This strategic intent is an obsession with winning on a global scale; it is clear about the outcome but flexible about the means of achieving that outcome. In this respect, these authors agree with the conventional wisdom. But then they say that the strategic intent cannot be realized either through long-term plans to build on existing competitive advantages or through the undirected process of "intrapreneurship" or use of autonomous small task forces often proposed by the critics of planning. Instead, they claim, the only route to success is through innovation and accelerated organizational learning because no competitive advantage is inherently sustainable. Successful companies focus on leveraging their resources; that is, they use what they have in new and innovative ways to build up a number of core competences and reach seemingly unattainable goals.

The less successful, on the other hand, focus on maintaining a strategic fit between their capability and market demands. This leads them to limit their ambitions to those that can be met with available resources. They focus on product/market units rather than core competences. They preserve consistency through conforming to financial objectives rather than through an emotive strategic intent. The route they follow is that of using generic strategies to secure competitive advantages that they believe to be inherently sustainable.

While the first mental model of strategy leads to innovation and organizational transformation, according to the authors, the second leads to repetition and imitation. The key difference between these models is that successful managers are not simply matching their resources to the requirements of the environment, leaving others to meet the requirements that their resources are incapable of delivering. Instead, they are finding innovative uses for their resources, thereby creating demands that they then find a way to meet. This view clearly questions the idea that successful organizations are those that fit or adapt to their environments. While these authors adhere to much of the stable equilibrium model, they thus strongly question one of its central propositions.

Understanding Complex Systems

Other research takes this process of questioning a stage further. Peter Senge's study of a number of companies (Hanover Insurance,

Herman Miller, People Express Airline, and others) explains success and failure in terms of the ability of organizations to learn.[8] One of the keys to an organization's learning capability is the ability of its managers to think in terms of complex system behavior. Senge's argument is that an organization is a complex system with something of a life of its own: the system itself can produce unexpected outcomes that managers did not intend. Managers will be unable to understand and cope effectively with this fact unless they are aware of the system's structure and the behavior patterns it produces. These ideas actually have been around since at least the 1950s,[9] but they have had little impact on the way most people in the business world think. Senge emphasizes the importance of this kind of thinking in improving the ability of managers to cope with turbulent change.

One way of understanding the systems approach to organizations is to examine the behavior of a supply chain. For example, a beer factory supplies a number of distributors, who then ship the beer to an even larger number of retailers. Orders for beer flow back upstream from retailers to distributors and from them to the factory. The factory, the distributors, and the retailers form a system consisting of flows of orders in one direction and flows of beer in the other. Each part of the system tries to ship beer as fast as possible and maintain inventories at minimum levels without running out of beer to sell, because this is how each individual can maximize profits.

However, because of its very nature—the feedback impact of the behavior of one component of the system (distributors, for example) on another (retailers, for example) and the lags in information flow between them—this system shows a marked tendency to amplify minor ordering disturbances at the retail end of the supply chain. An initial 10 percent increase in orders at the retail level thus can eventually cause production at the factory to peak at 40 percent above its starting level and then collapse.

Senge reports how he has used this example as a game with thousands of groups of managers in many countries. Even when managers know about the likely consequences of this system's behavior, he has always found that a small increase in demand at the retail level leads to increasingly amplified demands at later stages in the supply chain. This happens because there is a time delay between the placing of larger orders and the delivery of increased supplies of beer. During this time period, when, say, retailers are shipping out more than they are receiving, their inventories decline. They therefore tend to overorder to restore optimal inventory levels. This behavior is repeated throughout the supply chain, leading to growing demand further up the supply chain that at least initially cannot be met.

Once the time lag has passed, beer arrives in great quantities. Incoming orders then suddenly decline because backlogs are reduced throughout the chain and people no longer overorder. Eventually almost all players end up with large inventories that they cannot unload. By being aware of the way the system as a whole functions, rather than simply concentrating on their own part of it, players in the beer game can avoid the extreme instabilities of these cycles. Try as they may, however, they cannot remove the cycles altogether.

This same kind of cyclical behavior can be seen in any business. Furthermore, the departments or other groupings within an organization can be modeled in much the same way. For example, we might study an organizational system consisting of connections between production, marketing, R&D, and finance departments. The principal lessons that all of these system models teach are the same.

First, the structure of the system influences behavior. In this sense the system has a life of its own, quite apart from what each of its individual components intentionally does. If we want to understand what is going on, therefore, it is not sufficient to examine the intentions and actions of each individual component. We must also understand those aspects of the total behavior that are due to the system as a whole, aspects that are beyond the ability of any single component on its own to control or even always to understand. The cycles in ordering, inventory levels, and production in the beer game are really the consequence of the structure of the system. No one intends or is to blame for these fluctuations, and no single component on its own can remove them.

Second, complex human systems often produce unexpected and even counterintuitive results. In the beer game, retailers increase orders above their real need, expecting this to lead to bigger deliveries. But because all retailers are doing this, and because of lags in information flows, the unexpected result is lower deliveries.

Third, in complex systems the links between cause and effect are distant in time and space. Thus, in the beer game the causes of increased demand appeared at the retail end of the supply chain, distant in space from the factory and distant in time because of the lags in order flows. Such distance between cause and effect makes it very difficult to say what is causing what. Those playing the beer game always think that the fluctuations in deliveries are being caused by fluctuations in customer demand, but in fact they are due to the manner in which the system operates. This means that it is extremely difficult to make accurate predictions of what will happen in a specific place over a specific time period.

Instead of specific predictions, Senge points out, simulations on computers can be used to identify general qualitative patterns of behavior—sometimes called templates or archetypes—that will be similar to those we are likely to experience in reality, although they never will be exactly the same.

An example of the kind of pattern or archetype Senge is talking about is a very common one he calls "Limits to Growth." This occurs when a reinforcing positive feedback process is installed to produce a desired result (a positive growth loop) but inadvertently creates secondary effects (a negative limiting loop) that put a stop to the growth. The immediate response to this result is to push harder on the factors that cause growth. In fact, however, this is counterproductive because it causes the system to bump even more firmly against the inhibiting loop. The real solution is to work on the negative loop, on relaxing the inhibitors.

People Express Airline is an example of this pattern in action. This airline provided an innovative low-cost service between the United States and Europe and within the United States. This was a "no frills" service, but it was reliable. It proved to be very popular, and demand grew rapidly. People Express found that it could not build up even its limited service capacity fast enough to keep pace with the exploding demand, and reliability consequently declined. Instead of slowing its growth (by increasing prices) and focusing on training to increase service capacity, it continued to grow as fast as it could. Service levels declined more and more rapidly, staff morale failed, and competition became more fierce. Eventually customers no longer found People Express reliable enough, and the business collapsed.

The purpose of examining archetypes such as this is to recondition perceptions so that managers are able to perceive the structures at play, the dynamic patterns of behavior involved, and the potential leverage in those structures. The archetypes or templates are meant to be used in a flexible way to help understand patterns in events. They are analogies that can be used in building a new explanation of each specific situation confronted. As Senge puts it, "The art of systems thinking lies in being able to recognize increasingly (dynamically) complex and subtle structures . . . amid the wealth of details, pressures and cross currents that attend all real management settings. In fact, the essence of mastering systems thinking as a management discipline lies in seeing patterns where others see only events and forces to react to."[10]

The fourth lesson of systems dynamics is that complex systems are highly sensitive to some changes but remarkably insensitive to others. Such systems contain influential pressure, or leverage, points. If we can influence those points, we can have a major impact on the behavior of the system. The trouble is that these points are difficult to identify. In the beer game the leverage point lies in the ordering practices of retailers and distributors. By acting at that point, players can damp down the cycles. Unfortunately, the pressure points from which favorable chain reactions can be initiated are extremely difficult to find and may well be outside one's own organization.

Usually, it seems, complex systems are insensitive to changes and indeed counteract and compensate for externally applied correctives. If they respond to policy changes at all, they often do so in ways opposite to what the policymakers intended. Thus, when retailers find that deliveries from the distributors are curtailed, they respond by ordering even more and so make the situation worse. Because of this natural tendency to counteract and compensate—that is, to move to stability—it is necessary to change the system itself rather than simply apply externally generated remedies.

These lessons point to the conclusion that, because an organization is a complex system, attempts to plan its long-term future and design changes in its culture and behavior patterns are likely to prompt counterforces and therefore to lead to either little change or unexpected and undesirable changes. The future of a single component of the beer supply chain, for example, could not possibly be planned in isolation from the other components. Plans would stand a chance of being realized only if all the firms in the supply chain cooperated in a joint plan, and the regulatory authorities would soon have something to say about that. This kind of systems thinking leads us to suspect that the very structure of a complex system makes planning its specific long-term future virtually impossible.

Senge's explanation of how companies succeed falls within the stable equilibrium model in a few respects. He attaches great importance to the shared vision, which he defines as an emotional force related to the future that managers wish to create. He talks about enrolling and enlisting people to commit to the vision. He sees harmony and consensus as essential elements of successful organizations. However, he also makes it clear that such visions emerge from contention and dialogue between many individuals, rather than being the intention of one charismatic leader. His analysis counters simple ideas of top-down control and cohesive teams. His picture of successful organizations incorporates irregularity and unpredictability as essential characteristics.

Avoiding Stable Equilibrium

Further research into business success and failure erodes the stable equilibrium view of organizational success in yet other ways. For example, Danny Miller's investigation leads him to conclude that many companies fail because of the "Icarus paradox."

> The fabled Icarus of Greek mythology is said to have flown so high, so close to the sun, that his artificial wax wings melted and he plunged into the Aegean sea. The power of Icarus's wings gave rise to the abandon that doomed him. The paradox, of course, is that his greatest asset led to his demise. And that same paradox applies to many outstanding companies to-

day: their victories and their strengths often seduce
them into excesses that cause their downfall. Success
leads to specialization and exaggeration, to confidence
and complacency, to dogma and ritual.[11]

Miller detects four configurations of organizational structures, strategies, styles, and systems that have led to success. He also
identifies four trajectories organizations follow as they extend and
amplify these configurations until they fail:

- The focusing trajectory takes Craftsmen organizations (those
  with strong engineering and tight operational controls as their
  major source of competitive advantage) and turns them into
  Tinkerers (insular firms whose technocratic culture alienates
  customers with perfect but irrelevant offerings). By focusing on
  their quality or cost leadership strategies and their engineering
  and operational strengths, these companies come to ignore their
  customers. Periods in the history of Digital, Disney, Caterpillar,
  and Texas Instruments illustrate this path.
- The venturing trajectory converts entrepreneurial Builders
  (high-growth companies managed by imaginative leaders and
  creative planning staffs) into Imperialists (companies overtax-
  ing their resources by expanding too rapidly into businesses
  they know little about). Examples here are provided by ITT,
  Litton Industries, Gulf and Western, Dome Petroleum.
- The inventing trajectory along which Pioneers (companies with
  excellent R&D departments, flexible think tank operations, and
  state-of-the-art products) move to become Escapists (run by cults
  of scientists who squander resources in the pursuit of grandiose
  futuristic inventions). Examples here are Federal Express,
  Wang, Apple, Rolls Royce, and Polaroid.
- The decoupling trajectory that transforms Salesmen (companies
  with developed marketing skills, broad markets, and prominent
  brand names) into Drifters (companies whose sales fetish ob-
  scures design issues and who become aimless and bureaucratic,
  producing me-too offerings). Examples here are Procter & Gam-
  ble, General Motors, and IBM.

The pathway from initial success to ultimate failure that Miller identifies in his sample of companies is quite clearly generated by an amplifying feedback process. It is a self-reinforcing pattern of circular behavior that initially constitutes a virtuous circle but ultimately develops into a vicious one. Those ultimately vicious circles also clearly move companies in two different directions. The focusing and decoupling trajectories take a company to more and more integrated, centrally controlled, and orderly positions—stable equilibrium. The venturing and inventing trajectories take an organization to more and more differentiated and decentralized positions—unstable equilibrium. This conclusion is a major challenge to the idea that successful organizations are those that tend toward stable equilibrium. On the contrary, it suggests that stable equilibrium should be avoided.

Seeking Nonequilibrium and Tension

Richard Pascale[12] reaches very similar conclusions, and he takes the analysis further in a number of ways. He explains the continuing success of Honda and the transformation of Ford Motor Company in the 1980s, as well as the success and failure of a number of other companies, in terms of the following model. According to him, successful organizations are characterized by a paradox. On the one hand, they have to achieve "fit," a state of coherence, centralization, tight control, synergy, and adaptation to the environment. Organizations clearly need "fit" if they are to conduct an orderly day-to-day business. But at the same time, successful organizations also need "split." "Split" means giving individuals freedom to act, decentralizing, differentiating, promoting variety and rivalry. Organizations need "split" because without it they cannot develop new perspectives and innovative actions. Developing new perspectives means shattering old perspectives and changing old structures—creativity requires destruction.[13] The need for an organization simultaneously to display "fit" and "split" creates tension, but that tension is creative because it provokes inquiry and questioning. That tension leads to the learning organization, with its continual dialogue between contradicting points of view.

Tension leads to what Pascale calls "contend," the positive

use of tension and conflict to create and generate new perspectives. Through this clash of opposites the organization "transcends" to a new constellation of "fit" and "split." This view of organizational development is a dialectical one in which contradictory forces produce, through learning, a new synthesis of more complex strategies and structures. Organizations use fit and split at the same time to produce sudden jumps to new positions and postures. Pascale stresses the need to orchestrate, rather than balance, the extremes of fit and split that lead to excess and failure to preserve the tension rather than move to either stable or unstable equilibrium. The paradox is that organizations have to use both ends of the "fit/split" spectrum at once; that is, the choices facing an organization are "both/and," not "either/or."

Noticeably absent from this explanation of how businesses succeed are the master plan, the charismatic leader, and the overarching vision. Instead, new strategic directions are seen to emerge from many piecemeal actions. According to this explanation, continuing movement toward either the stable equilibrium of "fit" or the unstable equilibrium of "split" is failure. Success lies away from equilibrium in a state of contradiction between stability and instability, tight and flexible controls, centralized and decentralized structures. Success has to do with the ability of an organization to sustain and manage contradiction and tension.

The Pascale and Miller studies present explanations of organizational development based on circular processes that amplify small changes and generate patterns of change in the form of unstable vicious and virtuous circles. They identify organizational learning as the process by which successful managers deal with this instability. Their approach provides a far better match with the global competition game discussed earlier than today's dominant explanation of success as an orderly, predictable movement toward stable equilibrium.

Replacing the Stable Equilibrium Mind-Set

Over the past few years, then, a number of important studies have presented evidence and explanations that undermine one aspect or another of the vision/plan model of strategic management and the associated idea that success is a state of stable equilibrium.

- The notion that successful companies stick to what they know best and adapt to their environment is rejected in favor of the principle of creative interaction with other actors in the environment.
- The simple model of an organization as a group of people coherently pursuing a preset goal gives way to the model of an organization as a complex system with a life of its own, where cause and effect are distant from each other and outcomes are not only unintended but unexpected.
- The prescription that organizations should move toward ever greater stability is challenged by the observation that stable organizations ultimately fail. The prescription then becomes one of sustaining organizations in states of nonequilibrium in which tension, contradiction, and paradox all provoke learning.
- The assumption that it is possible to install comprehensive control systems and culture change programs to take a whole organization to success yields to acceptance of the fact that organizations are such complex systems that all managers can do is intervene at sensitive leverage points and change certain aspects of those organizations.

In the chapters that follow, I will argue that if we put these four points into the context of the discoveries scientists have made about nonlinear feedback systems, we will develop a new mind-set that will guide strategic management away from equilibrium. The feedback system framework takes Senge's analysis a stage further and provides explanations for the business behavior observed by Miller and Pascale. This new mind-set gives greater insight into the question of whether new strategic directions can be organizationally intended or whether they can only emerge from the interactions between people in organizations. The new mind-set also has important implications for our understanding of control—whether it is possible to be "in control" of the long-term future of an innovative organization or whether we have to use some other notion of control. And finally, the new mind-set leads to different views of the role of shared cultures in organizational success and the nature of creativity in human systems.

Why Does the Vision-Plan Framework Fail?

Management experts operate in the same manner as other experts: when they interpret business situations in order to act, they employ mental models that they very rarely examine or question. For example, both the managers and the consultants at the company described earlier in this chapter were employing a particular model when they attempted to plan how to differentiate their company and its products from their competition. They assumed without question that success is to be secured by fixing on some vision or image, preparing plans to achieve it, and motivating people to believe it and cohere around it. Later on in the chapter we saw that researchers have discovered that managers do not use plans as part of a strategic control system, and those researchers employed the same mental model to explain why. They claimed that managers are in some sense performing inadequately because they are not setting clear long-term objectives, preparing long-term plans, and monitoring their progress against milestones. The real question, however, is whether the advice makes sense. When we consider the other research summarized in this chapter, we find that it does not and that we have to question the whole basis upon which this mind-set is built.

Underlying today's mental models is the unquestioned assumption that observed effects can be directly linked to causes in a straightforward, linear fashion—that our actions and their outcomes can be, in principle at least, unequivocally connected to each other. This basic assumption leads to a number of beliefs that govern what we look for when we research, what we prescribe, and what management actions we design. These beliefs include the following:

- A successful organization is moving toward stable equilibrium.
- Techniques and systems can be installed in advance to secure innovative success.
- Strategic thinking is an analytical process.

- Strategy is a regular pattern of action flowing from organizational intention.
- Control is negative feedback that keeps the organization on a predetermined, regular path.
- More innovative activity can be secured when people are encouraged to participate through flexible structures, loose job definitions, and distributed power.

As soon as we undermine the basic assumption about cause and effect, as the modern science of nonlinear dynamics does, then we destroy each of these ideas. The ideas are discussed separately in the six chapters that follow, showing how a mind-set produced by modern understandings of the complexity of dynamic systems leads to the opposite perspective in each case. This new mind-set leads us to see that long-term plans serve only as a rational defense against the anxiety provoked by great uncertainty. Visions and shared values are mystic versions of the same defense. The new perspective leads us to abandon these defenses and focus our attention instead on improving the learning and political interaction that constitute real strategic management, the mode successful managers actually use to undertake innovative journeys of exploration into the unknowable future.

3

Stable Instability: Creating the Far-from-Equilibrium Organization

A common theme runs through the way the media treat just about all businesses these days. The media build a company's top managers into business folk heroes as long as the firm's performance improves rapidly. As soon as performance falters, however, the media knock the "heroes" down again. During the mid 1980s, newspapers in the United Kingdom were full of praise for the business folk heroes of the Thatcher era. These included Ralph Halpern, who transformed sleepy Hepworths into a modern chain of men's fashion stores; George Davies, who developed the Next chain of fashion stores, focusing specifically on customers in their late teens and early twenties; and Alan Sugar, who built up the Amstrad consumer electronics empire. Today Hepworths and Next, together with their principal architects, are seen as has-beens. Alan Sugar and Amstrad come in for periodic criticism as well.

The same phenomenon occurs in the United States. Ford Motor Company is praised for its business skill during some periods and written off in others. General Electric is held up as a model for all to follow in some eras and derided as an overweight conglomerate during others. The criteria for media praise and condemnation are clear. Companies and their managers are seen as excellent only when they display consistently stable improvements in their performance.

The Accepted View: Excellence Equals Stability

It is not only sensation-seeking newspapers and television programs that interpret excellence as consistency in performance. Those who

43

seriously try to identify what makes a successful business usually use the same criterion. One of the best-known examples is Peters and Waterman's book *In Search of Excellence.*[1] Peters and Waterman identified a number of companies that were widely regarded as "state of the art" in management terms. These were companies, such as Boeing, Du Pont, Kodak, Atari, and Avon, that had shown consistent improvement in profitability as well as continuing innovative product and technology development. The authors identified common features in the management practice of those companies and then prescribed the installation of those features in other companies that sought excellence.

But within five years, two-thirds of the chosen companies could no longer be described as excellent: consistent profit and product improvement had faltered. At the time of the study, for example, IBM was regarded as an excellent company. A few years later it was widely judged to be "dead." By the late 1980s, however, it was once again being presented as a shining example to the rest of the business world.

Does it make sense continually to change our judgment in this way? To answer this question, we need to think more deeply about the nature of instability and why we equate it with failure.

Causes of Instability: Is Instability Always Bad?

The fact that we equate stability with excellence also affects the way we think about instability. Since we see instability as bad, we assume that it must be caused by some kind of failure on the part of business managers, either incompetence or ignorance. We naturally also assume, therefore, that removing these causes will remove instability and thus guarantee excellence or success.

Incompetence

Most business commentators, whether television "experts" or more serious analysts, tend to assume that irregularities in a company's performance are due to the incompetence of the business's top management team. This view is shared by many equity holders and top managers themselves. Any serious faltering in performance is therefore usually followed rapidly by a change in chief executive and key members of the board. Following this assumption that irregular business performance is primarily a consequence of incompetence, we look for the organizational structures, control systems, cultures, management styles, and leadership characteristics that constitute competence—that is, that lead to stability. We draw the conclusion that if we can identify the elements of competence and install them, we will be able largely to banish unstable business performance.

In the United Kingdom this identification of management competencies is being put on a formal footing by the Management Charter Initiative, which is supported by some of the major companies in the country. This initiative has identified what are regarded as the key competencies required at different levels in the management hierarchy. Management education programs are being designed to develop managers with the necessary competencies. The excellence of the country's businesses is expected to increase as a result.

Ignorance

We know, of course, that even if we do succeed in comprehensively identifying and installing the elements of competence, we still will not banish performance instability altogether. Future changes in markets and other aspects of the business environment cannot be forecast with complete accuracy. Every business therefore will be hit from time to time by unforeseen, random shocks from its environment. Oil prices may rise and fall in unexpected ways, for example; so may interest and exchange rates. Customer requirements and technologies may also develop in unforeseen ways.

Under these circumstances, unstable business performance will be generated by what amounts to ignorance. But ignorance can be conquered, to some extent at least, by gathering and processing more information, applying more sophisticated forecasting techniques, and conducting more research. Competent managers are expected to seek to overcome ignorance as far as they are able. They will turn as many apparently random shocks as possible into predictable events and design responses before the events occur. Competent managers, we believe, think about the future and follow logical steps to deal with it. They try to secure stability by banishing ignorance.

The Nature of Nonlinear Feedback

The discovery of the complex behavior of dynamic systems, referred to in Chapter One, must lead us to challenge the view that irregular business performance is due solely to incompetence and ignorance. When the behavior of a system is driven by certain kinds of feedback mechanisms, that behavior may be unstable purely because of the nature or structure of those feedback mechanisms. Furthermore, far from being the enemy of success, this particular kind of limited instability is vital to the ability of the system to be continually creative.

A comment on the possibility of a system being creative might be in order at this point. In Chapter Two, in the example of the beer game, we saw how it was quite realistic to talk about a system having a life of its own, generating behavior that is different from what any of its components intends or does. There we were talking about a human system, but the same point could just as easily apply to a system in nature. For example, the patterns of behavior in the weather are driven by a system that feeds this second's conditions (humidity, pressure, and wind speed, for example) into a set of laws that generate the next second's conditions. The system operates automatically through a process of repeatedly feeding back existing conditions into the same laws over and over again. No agent, either inside or outside the system, is controlling it, and it follows no master plan. In this sense, the system has a life of its own. Furthermore, the weather system generates patterns of specific behavior that are always different, and in this sense, it is a continually creative system. We can accurately describe any system as creative if it automatically generates continually different patterns of behavior. Scientists these days talk about feedback systems in nature making choices and behaving in creative ways.

The discovery that scientists have made about feedback systems is that it is necessary to sustain a system in the conditions in which limited instability occurs, rather than trying to remove it. Without such instability, the system will be incapable of developing new, innovative forms of behavior. It will be trapped into endlessly repeating its past and present behavior.

This discovery means that if a business system is driven by these kinds of feedback mechanisms, its performance could be unstable for reasons involving its very structure. Even if we could totally banish both incompetence and ignorance, the business's performance would still display instability. Furthermore, a business would have to exhibit instability if it was to be innovative. Systems, structure, success, and instability would be intimately interconnected. We would have to think of a business organization as a system with something of a life and a creative potential of its own, not subject in any simple way to individual human intention and control.

If these scientific discoveries have anything to do with business, they will force us to examine our most fundamental views about the requirements for business success. They would mean that the judgment that IBM is "excellent" one year and "dead" the next is not only trivial but dangerously misleading. We should expect, even require, an excellent company to have ups and downs in performance and display signs of instability simply because of its nature and its need to innovate. No amount of information gathering, analysis, research, or planning could alter this necessary instability. Neither could giving the company's managers all the competencies in the world.

It is important, then, to consider whether a business is a feedback system, and if so, whether it is the kind of feedback system to which this new understanding of complex dynamics applies. If a business is such a feedback system, it becomes vital to identify the conditions under which it will display inherent structural instability and to examine the question of whether such instability leads to business success.

These considerations are of practical importance because the actions managers design depend on what they believe about the nature of success. If they believe that instability is an inherent and necessary feature of a successful business, they will seek to provoke certain kinds of instability. If, on the other hand, they believe that instability is the enemy of success and is due simply to incompetence and ignorance, they will seek to banish all forms of instability.

And if they make the wrong judgment in this regard, their organization will not survive.

A Business as a Nonlinear Feedback System

It is not difficult to see that every organization is a web of feedback loops. Every business uses the cash flow generated by its past sales to purchase what it needs to carry out its present activities. Those activities, in turn, create the sales that generate the cash flow required for future value-adding activities. Cash moves in a loop over time, with inflows being fed back into outflows that in turn generate new inflows.

The same point applies to output. Part of yesterday's output is siphoned off to meet orders, and the rest feeds into inventories (or backlogs), which play an important part in determining output levels today. When inventories rise, a business cuts output levels; when backlogs (unfilled orders) rise, it raises output levels. Similarly, today's output feeds back into inventories (or backlogs) and affects decisions about tomorrow's output level. Output, then, also moves in a loop over time that connects the level in one period to that in another.

In fact, every performance indicator of a business is generated by a feedback loop because each is interconnected with all the others, and all are subject to time lags. Conducting a business, then, is simply moving around a large number of interconnected sales, output, input, cash flow, and profit feedback loops.

Business performance over time is driven by feedback mechanisms. But are these feedback mechanisms the type to which the new discoveries of complex dynamics apply?

The answer is yes. To see this, consider what most managers would call the most important feedback loop of all: profit. The profit that a company earns in a past time period plays an important part in the decisions about product offerings made in the present period. Typically, managers decide to plough back the profit of the previous period into present expenditures, which in turn result in product offerings during this or some future time period. Thus, previous profit is ploughed back into working capital, capital expenditure, R&D, advertising and promotion, and so on. The profit ploughed back may be bolstered by borrowing, and the capacity to do this will be related in some way to profitability. Profit in a previous period therefore leads, through a decision-making process, to product offerings in the present.

Those product offerings, in turn, lead to the profit of this period, the link being provided by the response of customers, competitors, and suppliers to that product offering and its input requirements. Relationships between a business and the organizations and people that constitute its environment therefore determine the profit that product offerings will yield. That profit will be fed back into the loop to determine the product offerings to be made in the next period, and so on. This loop is depicted in Figure 3.1, where P_{t-1} stands for profit in the last period, E_t for expenditure in this period, and P_t for profit in this period.

If managers ploughed back a constant proportion of profit into, say, working capital and the consequent output of product, in turn, always brought in a constant proportion of profit, then profit in one period would bear a direct proportional relationship to profit in the next. For example, suppose managers always plough back 1.2 times last period's profit into working capital. Suppose also that this working capital always results in a profit of 1.5 times that working capital. If the starting level of profit for this company is 100, working capital in the next period will be 120, and it will

Figure 3.1. The Profit Feedback Loop.

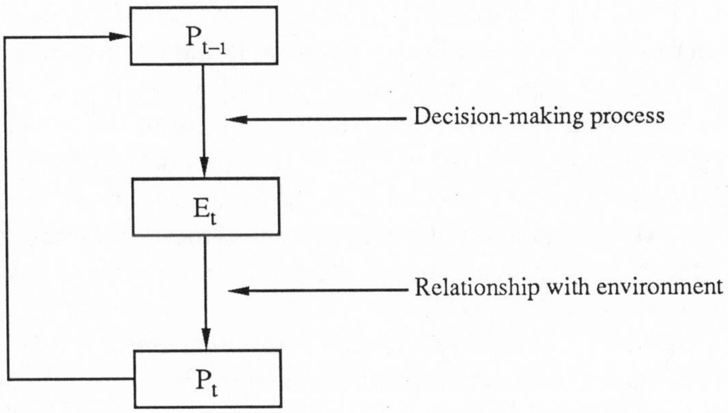

yield profit of 180. The period after that will see a further 80 percent increase in profit, and so on.

Of course, such simple linear relationships do not occur in the real business world. First, managers do not simply plough back a constant proportion of profit into each expenditure category. They know quite well that the more extra money they put into R&D for example, the smaller the additional benefits each extra dollar brings (the economists' law of diminishing returns). Appropriate decision-making rules are then such that the more managers allocate to R&D this period, the smaller the additional amounts they are likely to allocate in the next period. The same applies to advertising, capital expenditure, working capital, and most other expenditure categories.

Second, managers will be prevented from following simple decision rules of proportional allocation by financing constraints, limited capacity, and shortages of materials and skilled labor.

Third, relationships between a company and its environment are such that increases in output do not bring in proportional increases in profit. The more product a business offers, the less additional profit it will bring because the business will have to lower prices to encourage extra demand.

Fourth, customers and competitors do not respond to price and product offering changes in a simple proportional manner—they under- and overreact. Nor do managers react to customer and competitor responses in a simple proportional way—they too under- and overreact.

The relationship between profit in one period and profit in another must therefore be nonproportional, that is, nonlinear. The profit feedback loop is nonlinear because its operation is constrained by fundamental economic laws of supply and demand, diminishing returns, and economies and diseconomies of scale. The profit feedback loop is also constrained by limitations on finance, capacity, skills, and many more. And perhaps most important of all, every feedback loop in an organization will be nonlinear because of human behavior.

It is not just performance indicators that are linked by nonlinear feedback loops. Almost all interactions in organizations between individuals, or groups of individuals, take on a nonlinear feedback form. For example, a manager may alter some minor working condition in his department. That action feeds back into the responses of staff, who may send a delegate to protest. The manager may react with greater determination to impose his will. The response may be a strike. An organization is a vast web of nonlinear feedback loops.

The discoveries scientists have made about structural instability and complex dynamics apply to almost all nonlinear feedback loops, the exceptions being very minor. These discoveries must therefore, potentially at least, have something to say about the operation of business systems because every business is a web of nonlinear feedback loops. Before discussing these discoveries further, however, it will be helpful to consider how feedback loops work.

Feedback and Equilibrium

There are two forms of feedback, negative and positive—that is, feedback that damps the behavior of a system and feedback that amplifies it. We normally see these as two distinct forms of feedback—and consequent behavior—that present a system with an "either/or" choice: negative feedback and stable equilibrium, or positive feedback and unstable equilibrium—being "in control," or going "out of control."

Negative Feedback and Stable Equilibrium

Negative or damping feedback is widely used for automatic control or regulation. Frequently cited examples of negative feedback include the central heating control system in a house and the governor on a steam engine. In the case of heating control, a desired temperature is set in the control mechanism, which also contains a device to sense the room temperature. When the room temperature falls below the desired level, the control sensor detects this, and the control system turns the heat on. When the temperature rises above the desired level, the opposite happens. By responding to each deviation from the desired level in an opposite or negative way, the control system damps any movement away from the desired level. The controls thus keep the room temperature close to a stable level over time.

The same principle applies to the steam engine governor. As the boiler is stoked, steam pressure rises and the engine speeds up. The governor responds to this by opening a valve to release the steam and so pull the engine speed back to a desired level. As soon as the speed falls below the desired level, the valve closes, causing steam pressure to rise and the engine speed to increase to the desired level. Here, too, the control system damps fluctuations around the desired level and preserves predictable stable equilibrium.

The short-term control system of a business is quite clearly a feedback mechanism. Managers almost always think about it in terms of negative, damping feedback. Thus they fix targets for profits and then prepare their annual plans or budgets, setting out the time path for product volumes, prices, and costs that will yield those profit targets. The plans also determine the actions to be taken to secure these volumes, prices, and cost levels. As the business moves through time, outcomes are measured and compared with the plan projections to yield variances or deviations. Frequent monitoring of those variances prompts corrective action to bring performance indicators back onto their planned paths. To be sure, time lags and unforeseen environmental changes ensure that the adjustments are never perfect. But when the control system is operating effectively, as it would in an excellent company, actual output should fluctuate around the planned levels in a tightly constrained manner. The scheduling, budgetary, and planning control system of a business thus is designed to use negative feedback in exactly the same way as a central heating control or a steam engine governor. The outcome, too, is intended to be the same: the business is kept in equilibrium on a stable, predetermined path.

Positive Feedback and Explosively Unstable Equilibrium

Positive or amplifying feedback operates in exactly the opposite manner. If it were used in a heating system or a steam engine, the system would develop along a self-reinforcing path that took temperature or engine speed further and further away from the desired level. A tiny increase in temperature above the desired level would turn on the heat, thus increasing the deviation—that is, making the room temperature rise even further. In the case of the steam engine, a small increase in engine speed would partly close the valve, raising steam pressure and thus engine speed. The valve would then be closed even further, further increasing steam pressure and engine speed until the engine blew up.

In short, positive feedback escalates small changes. The behavior of a system driven by such amplifying feedback will always move into a self-reinforcing vicious or virtuous circle—it will become "runaway" or "explosive" unless it is limited in some way. The paths that a system driven by positive feedback will follow are predictable—the system is thus in equilibrium but of a highly unstable kind.

Businesses may also display amplifying feedback of an unlimited kind that produces harmful results. For example, a service department faced with increasing response times to telephone calls may divert resources from answering letters to answering calls. Then, however, the letter backlogs rise, and more irate customers phone in to demand replies to their letters. Telephone response times consequently rise even further. More resources are diverted to deal with the problem, and so the amplification continues. It will continue until someone steps in to stop it; it has no inbuilt limit and is therefore potentially explosively unstable. Compound rates of growth are another example of the amplifying feedback businesses experience. This usually virtuous circle always causes problems unless it is restrained or damped in some way—recall the People Express example of too rapid growth given in Chapter Two. Effective controls keep growth within limits that can be handled.

No sane engineer designs engine or heating control systems to act through positive feedback and set off on predictably unstable paths to explosion. Similarly, no sane manager designs business control systems that lead to increasingly divergent behavior until the organization disintegrates. We therefore almost always think of control systems, including those of business, in terms of negative or damping feedback designed to produce regular patterns of behavior.

Bounded Instability Far from Equilibrium

The key discovery about the operation of nonlinear feedback loops is that stable equilibrium and explosively unstable equilibrium are not the only endpoints of behavior open to such systems. Nonlinear systems have a third choice: a state of bounded or limited instability, far from equilibrium, in which behavior has a pattern, but it is irregular. This kind of instability is produced because the system's structure is such that when the system is far enough away from equilibrium, it continually flips between negative and positive feedback. This means that the choice of far-from-equilibrium behavior is a "both/and" one because the system is driven alternatively by both positive and negative feedback and the outcome is both stable and unstable. And it is so driven not because some agent within or outside it applies first one kind of feedback and then the other but because the nonlinear structure of the loop causes this to happen autonomously in an apparently random way. Nonlinearity is in a sense its own constraint, and stable instability is one of its fundamental properties. The choice of equilibrium behavior, on the other hand, is an "either/or" one. Either the system is driven by negative feedback and then tends to stable equilibrium or the system is driven by positive feedback and then tends to unstable equilibrium. To stop that instability, some agent or condition outside the system would have to "step in and put a stop to it."

Chaotic Behavior: A Third State

To summarize, any given nonlinear feedback system (loop or mechanism) can operate in a negative feedback manner to produce stable equilibrium behavior, or it can be driven by positive feedback to generate explosively unstable equilibrium behavior, or finally, it can operate in a mode in which feedback autonomously flips between positive and negative feedback to produce behavior that is both stable and unstable. What relationship do these states of behavior bear to each other? We can see the relationship if we think of a given feedback system being driven to behave more and more responsively and sensitively.

When a nonlinear feedback system is driven away from the peaceful state of stable equilibrium toward the hectic equilibrium of explosive instability, it passes through a phase of bounded instability in which it displays highly complex behavior. We might think of this phase as a border area between stable equilibrium and unstable equilibrium. This border area is a state of paradox in which two contradictory forces, stability and instability, are operating simultaneously, pulling the system in different directions. While the system is in this border area, neither of these contradictory forces can be removed; instead, the forces are endlessly rearranged in different yet similar patterns. (The reader will recall from Chapter Two the explanation Pascale gives of how successful businesses develop: the endless reconfiguring of the opposing forces of "fit" and "split.") When the system is in the border area, it never behaves in a regular way that leads to equilibrium. Instead, it generates patterns of behavior that are not only irregular but also absolutely unpredictable. Nonetheless, such behavior has an overall, "hidden," qualitative pattern.

Scientists have called this combination of specific unpredictability and qualitative pattern chaos, fractal, or strange. Only when a system operates in this chaotic, fractal, far-from-equilibrium state is it continually creative in the sense that as its behavior is automatically fed back into the rule that generates it, different outcomes are always produced. Equilibrium states are ones of predictable repetition that by definition exclude continuing creativity, while chaos is a state of endless variety that is creativity. The tension generated by being pulled in contradictory directions, the paradox of control and freedom, leads to such bounded instability and creativity.

The Mandelbrot Set: A Picture of Chaos

We can begin to understand chaos intuitively by looking at a map of the stability and instability conditions called the Mandelbrot set.[2] To draw this map, a computer must make many thousands of calculations using a particular nonlinear feedback relationship. Simply imagine plugging any number into this feedback relationship. Because the computer is using a feedback loop to calculate, this starting number will generate another number that will then be fed back automatically into the loop to generate yet another number, and so on. The computer will churn out a sequence of numbers until it is told to stop. Then we pick out some other number and have the computer repeat the whole process once more. We do this for thousands of starting numbers, thus generating thousands of sequences.

We will discover that some of the sequences rapidly become stable and orderly, settling down into predictable patterns over time—patterns either of constancy or of perfectly regular cycles. In other words, those starting numbers generate sequences that reach stable equilibrium. Other starting numbers generate sequences that rapidly grow explosively to infinity in a perfectly predictable way— that is, they reach the equilibrium of explosive instability. The normal expectation is that a system is either stable or unstable. We would therefore expect to find that every starting number we select rapidly becomes either stable or unstable. We would expect to find a clear-cut border between stability and instability with starting numbers clearly on one side or the other. Such a border would, then, not be of any real interest because it would merely be a line separating two classes of events. That indeed was the expectation of mathematicians before Mandelbrot mapped the border area between stability and instability for the feedback relationship we are talking about.

To draw this map, the computer can be instructed to plot, say, black points for all starting numbers that produce a stable sequence and white points for all those that we can rapidly conclude will generate an unstable sequence. This will produce a map of all the starting conditions leading to stability and all the immediately obvious starting conditions leading to instability, the two final states that we expect this particular nonlinear feedback system to be attracted to (the two attractors for the system).

The result of doing this is shown in Figure 3.2. The black blob in the middle represents all starting events that yield stable outcomes (attraction to stable equilibrium) and the large white area outside this blob represents events that lead rapidly to instability (attraction to explosively unstable equilibrium). In this first attempt to draw the map, all points are clearly quite separate from each other, being either black or white, stable or unstable. According to this map, our system appears to have a clear-cut choice only between being attracted to stability or being attracted to instability. This, however, is an appearance only, due to the fact that we have

Figure 3.2. A Rough Plot of the Mandelbrot Set.

Source: Penrose, R. *The Emperor's New Mind.* Oxford, England: Oxford University Press, 1989. By permission of Oxford University Press.

not paid enough detailed attention to the border area between those events leading to stability and those leading to instability.

Behavior at the Border

We get a great surprise when we start to look closely at the border of the black figure—that is, the border between stability and instability. We discover that this border is not the clean-cut, clear line that we might have expected. Instead we discover that this border area pictures the third attractor for a nonlinear feedback system— bounded instability, far from equilibrium. (Of course, the map will look different for different nonlinear feedback systems, but the general properties of chaos are the same for all.)

We can see what this third attractor looks like on our computer map by taking smaller and smaller intervals between the starting
numbers at the border line and plotting their stability or instability
as we did before.[3] When we do this we find, as shown in Figure 3.3,
that the borders are complex, highly irregular, wispy lines.

Now suppose we get the computer to make thousands of
calculations for a small area of one of those wispy lines. The result
is complex patterns, an example of which is shown in the top half
of Figure 3.4. (The computer can be instructed to draw these pat-

Figure 3.3. A More Detailed Plot of the Mandelbrot Set.

Source: Penrose, R. *The Emperor's New Mind.* Oxford, England:
Oxford University Press, 1989. By permission of Oxford University Press.

Figure 3.4. Details of the Border Around the Mandelbrot Set.

Source: Penrose, R. *The Emperor's New Mind.* Oxford, England: Oxford University Press, 1989. By permission of Oxford University Press.

terns in color, with results of striking beauty.[4]) If we in turn explore
the detail of a part of this pattern, we will see other patterns embedded in it, such as the one shown in the bottom half of Figure
3.4. And in the middle of this detail, there is a black blob very
similar to the one we started with in the first place—an island of
stability in a sea of chaotic complexity. If we now start to explore
the borders around this island, we will discover further complex
patterns containing further islands of stability. And so we could go
on forever, probing more and more deeply into an infinitely deep
structure. Whenever we set the system off from a starting number
in the border area, the system will behave in the complex way
shown in the maps. Small changes in the starting numbers will lead
to different but recognizable chaotic patterns. It will take a more
substantial change in the starting numbers to get the system to
display the simple behavior of clear-cut stability or instability
again. In this sense, then, we may say that once the system enters
the border area, it will stay there unless a significant change or some
strong force pushes it either to stability or instability.

    In this map of the Mandelbrot set, what you see depends on
how closely you look, and it is different each time. But it is also
always similar: recognizably irregular patterns always appear. Tiny
differences in our perspective, tiny differences in the range of
numbers we focus on, lead to very different, yet recognizably similar
patterns.

    In this border area we cannot make clear-cut distinctions
between stability and instability because the starting conditions that
lead to one are so close to the starting conditions that lead to the
other. They are so close, in fact, that we could never measure or act
upon the differences between them: we could never determine in
advance which end condition was going to occur because we are
incapable of infinite precision. For all practical purposes, then,
instability and stability, irregularity and regularity, are hopelessly
intertwined with each other here.

    At the border between stability and instability, nonlinear
feedback systems generate a whole world of forms that are neither
stable nor unstable but a paradoxical combination of both. Their
variety and beauty are such that we can describe this mathematical
system as one that is continuously creative. If a system is not con-

scious and yet produces an endless stream of new and beautiful forms, it is just as creative as a conscious system doing the same thing. In the old mechanistic mind-set of the scientist, nature's systems were thought to behave in absolutely predictable, predetermined ways. From this perspective, it would be absurd to talk about a natural system choosing to behave in a particular way or creating something new. Choice and creativity are, from this perspective, confined to consciousness, and any order would be there by prior design. The new understanding is that nature's systems are driven by nonlinear feedback, and the understanding of how these systems function changes the whole mind-set: we can now see that inanimate systems can choose and be creative; order can emerge unpredictably from chaos without prior design. The point of great importance that emerges from the study of nonlinear systems is this: a system is creative not when all its components pull in the same direction but when they generate tension by pulling in contradictory directions.

Ideas of this kind are far from new. Many ancient mythologies incorporated them, and artists and philosophers have spoken about them for a very long time. Psychology and the social sciences contain similar ideas. But these ideas have tended to be on the fringes of Western thought about business, and they are certainly not part of the mental equipment of most practicing managers in the West. It is interesting to reflect, however, that Eastern mythologies and Eastern ways of thinking are far more in tune with the kind of paradoxical situations just described.

Chaos in Nature

It is astonishing that very simple, absolutely fixed mathematical equations can generate the complex dynamics we have been talking about. Even more astonishing, such equations prove to describe how many of nature's systems behave. The ideas just described have moved from the realms of mythology, art, philosophy, and the fringes of the social sciences to become part of "proper" science.

The weather system is one natural system that is driven by nonlinear feedback mechanisms and displays chaotic behavior. Tiny changes in air pressure in one part of the world, perhaps provoked by a butterfly flapping its wings, may be amplified through the system to produce hurricanes in another, distant place. The system escalates some selected minuscule changes into self-reinforcing circles of storms, heat waves, and other weather phenomena. Because of this, it is impossible to make long-term weather forecasts. But even though we can say nothing about specific long-term weather patterns, we know that, overall, these patterns will be similar to those experienced before. Weather patterns are bounded or constrained in the sense that the system does not allow some patterns in some areas. Snowstorms do not happen in the Sahara, nor do heat waves in the Arctic.

　　Chaotic behavior, driven by nonlinear feedback, has also been demonstrated in gases, chemical reactions, the movement of a driven pendulum, population changes, and many more phenomena in nature.[5] An institute has been set up in Santa Fe, New Mexico, to promote multidisciplinary research into complex systems, including economic systems, that may exhibit similar behavior. Edgar Peters of Agora Asset Management, Inc., and other researchers make a convincing case for chaos interpretations of the behavior of the capital and foreign exchange markets.[6]

　　In this book I argue that nonlinear dynamics and chaotic behavior apply literally to human business systems; they are not simply an analogy or a metaphor. If managers wish to adopt a scientific approach to understanding their organizations, they must now take account of the far-from-equilibrium behavior of nonlinear feedback systems because organizations are just such systems. Furthermore, I will argue that managers must operate in the chaos border area if they are to succeed. But before doing so, we need to explore in further detail what the properties of this chaos border area are.

Characteristics of Chaotic Behavior

Chaotic behavior has two important characteristics, already mentioned, that we need to explore in greater detail. At one level, it is inherently unpredictable, while at another level it displays a "hidden" pattern. Chaos in its scientific sense is not utter confusion. It is constrained, rather than explosive, instability. It is a combination of order and disorder in which patterns of behavior continually unfold in irregular but similar forms.

Inherent Unpredictability

It is possible to forecast the conditions under which chaotic behavior will occur in a nonlinear feedback system, provided that we can identify the form of the feedback rule driving the system. This is so because feedback rules have a fixed structure, and they generate behavior that passes through absolutely fixed stages from stable time paths through cycles to chaos, within which there are areas of stability, until finally it emerges into explosive instability. When a system is either stable or unstable, its short- and long-term futures are perfectly predictable. When it is in chaos, however, the short-term behavior of the system can be predicted because it takes time for small changes to escalate. But it is impossible, even in principle, to predict specific long-term outcomes.

When a system operates in chaos, it is highly sensitive to small changes. It amplifies tiny fluctuations or disturbances throughout the system, but in a complex way that leads to completely different, inherently unpredictable forms of behavior. Because tiny changes, so tiny that we could never hope to notice or measure them all, can so completely alter the behavior of the system, its long-term development depends in effect upon chance. It follows that complex patterns involving self-reinforcing virtuous and vicious circles will occur. Clear-cut connections between cause and effect are lost in the unpredictable unfolding of events. At the same time, the behavior of an individual component of a system can have a profound effect on the future of the whole system.

In short, there is not just one future to which this kind of system moves as the result of some external cause. Instead, there are many possible futures, and which emerges will depend upon the precise detail of what the system does and what the systems constituting its environments do. There is no point in trying to simulate this future to provide a range of likely outcomes; we would have to know all this precise detail in advance to get anywhere near the future that will emerge, and it is impossible to obtain that degree of detailed knowledge. The only use of simulation and scenario building is to practice or learn in advance how to handle general kinds of situations that might arise—knowing that the real situation is sure to be different from any of the projected ones. Simulations are useful as predictions of short-term behavior and for modeling the behavior of systems that are sufficiently close to some kind of equilibrium, but they have no long-term predictive power at all for systems far from equilibrium.

The loss of clear linkage between cause and effect produced by chaotic behavior is easy to see in business situations. Take, for example, the difficulty we have in accounting for the superior performance of Japanese companies and for the decline in British and American heavy industries. After years of research and libraries of books, there are still no universally accepted causes for these phenomena. We have only widely conflicting explanations.

Now, if this inherent unpredictability over the long term and this fuzzy connection between cause and effect were the only properties of chaos, and we were to find that businesses have chaotic dynamics, we would have real trouble in coping. But this is not all there is to chaos. The second important property of chaos is its "hidden" pattern.

"Hidden" Patterns

Chaos is not simply random, unstable behavior. Its instability is bounded: there are limits outside of which the time path does not move, even though behavior is random within those limits. Chaos is not runaway, explosive instability because it is constrained by the structure of the rule generating it: it may set off on an amplifying path, but soon it will autonomously flip to damping feedback. As a consequence, chaotic behavior has an overall pattern within which specific random outcomes occur. The distinction is the one that exists between a category and the individual items and events within that category. For example, there is a category we call snowflakes, all members of which have certain features, but within that category each individual snowflake is different. Each snowflake is clearly recognizable as such, yet it is also different from all others because it is shaped by its individual history. As it fell to earth, tiny differences in its experience of temperature and air impurities, compared to that of nearby snowflakes, became reflected in a unique pattern.

When a feedback system is in stable equilibrium, there is no fundamental distinction between a category and the individuals within that category. All individual items or events within the category are exactly the same: they are all adapted to the same environment in the same way. In a sense there are no individuals. But when behavior is chaotic, the distinction between a category and the individuals constituting it becomes important. The individuals are not all the same, they are merely similar enough to warrant inclusion in the category. Under these circumstances, we can talk about history repeating itself and yet always being different.

To see how this idea relates to the world of business, consider how competitive advantage is built up in certain geographical locations.[7] Patterns with features in common can be detected in the development of businesses around certain educational institutions, for example. Excellent research centers in the fields of microelectronics and information technology at Stanford and the University of California, Berkeley, together with the availability of skilled labor, played an important part in the development of "Silicon Valley" in California. The availability of such advanced technology made this an attractive location for electronics manufacturers in the early stages of that industry's development. These businesses in turn attracted component suppliers and other support companies. In this example, we see a feedback process through which a particular constellation of industries is built up and gains a particular set of competitive advantages.

A similar process occurred around Cambridge in the United Kingdom. Here, too, a fine research center played an important part in the initial attraction of electronics and information technology firms to a particular location. Feedback connections attracted other businesses, and a whole new industrial area was established. Similar developments arose between Reading and Bristol, for similar reasons. Yet the specific composition of the industries that grew up around San Francisco, around Cambridge, and between Reading and Bristol are quite different. For example, neither of the two areas in the United Kingdom contains much silicon chip manufacturing capability.

The process is the same in, for example, the development of industries relating to fashion clothing and shoes in Northern Italy around Milan. Here, as with the education-related geographical developments, some initial advantage attracts a small cluster of companies. Through feedback, support industries are attracted as well, and so the pattern develops.

We can detect and recognize the common features of these patterns of geographical economic development wherever they occur, but their specific form is unpredictable and depends to a significant extent on chance. Failed attempt after failed attempt by governments to establish such geographical concentrations artificially through planned industrial policies attest to this unpredictability. Just as we cannot predict the form of such economic developments, we cannot predict exactly how they will evolve over time, nor can we show direct causes for their appearance. The pattern that emerges depends on many small events with escalating effects.

The "hidden" pattern in chaotic behavior therefore consists of the essential features of the category, the features that all individuals in the category have more or less in common. We conclude that individuals belong to a category by identifying such similarity. But we could look at it another way and say that the criteria for inclusion relate to the degree of dissimilarity or irregularity. We would then include individuals in a category only if there was a constant or regular degree of irregularity between them—if they did not deviate from each other by more than a fixed limit. In chaotic patterns the individuals are never exactly the same but they are all regularly irregular. The key point is that the "hidden" patterns or category features are qualitative rather than quantitative. They are recognizable, but we cannot pin them down. For example, we are often able to recognize individuals as belonging to the same family, even though we cannot specify what common features allow us to draw this conclusion.

Does Chaotic Behavior Equal Business Success?

Since a business is a web of nonlinear feedback loops, it too must face the possibilities of stable equilibrium, unstable equilibrium, and chaotic behavior. But which of these forms of behavior leads to success?

As we have noted, the current view is that a successful business always operates as close as possible to stable equilibrium, demonstrating instability only because it is continually disturbed by random shocks from its environment. It overcomes such instability by swift reaction—that is, negative feedback—to adapt to the shocks and return to equilibrium as quickly as possible. In other words, successful systems are thought to damp down change because instability is seen as undesirable. According to this view, successful managers would avoid positive feedback with its runaway potential, and firms would not succeed simply because they got caught up for a time, partly by chance, in virtuous circles. In short, if stable equilibrium really equates to success, we would not expect to find self-reinforcing amplifying processes normally associated with success.

If chaotic behavior is associated with success, however, we would expect to find managers intentionally employing positive feedback and escalating some small changes, as well as employing negative feedback and damping other changes. Furthermore, we would expect to find that success is often best explained by small chance events that are amplified through management determination into virtuous circles that last for a while until some other chance event comes along to damp things down or set vicious circles off. In short, we would expect to find successful companies caught up in varying patterns of self-reinforcing virtuous and vicious circles, both intentionally and unintentionally, that managers are unable to remove. If chaotic behavior produces success, we would expect to find that companies fail when they get close to equilibrium states. Before considering the evidence for equating success and chaos, we need to be clear on what is meant by chaotic behavior in business.

Recognizing Chaotic Behavior

It would not be possible to walk into a company and immediately observe chaos in the scientific sense meant here. In a company with chaotic dynamics, we would see visible order, tight short-term controls, consistent delivery of quality products, meeting of time and cost targets. These would all be secured through damping forms of control, through negative feedback applied to affect the short-term consequence of events and actions. In other words, the visible behavior of a chaotic company would appear about the same as that of a company in stable equilibrium. We would not describe the dynamics as chaotic if we simply observe that there is no order at all, that is, managers running from one short-term crisis to another and failing to deliver products on time at the right quality and the right cost. Chaos in its scientific sense is not utter confusion or disorder.

Chaos in a business organization takes the form of contradiction: the simultaneous presence of opposing ways of behaving. It is evidenced, for example, by managers who operate budgetary forms of control to keep the organization stable, while at the same time engaging in amplifying forms of political activity in which they try to undermine the status quo. Chaos in its scientific sense takes the form of conflict, as when an organization experiences the clash of countercultures, the tensions of political activity, the contention and dialogue through which managers handle ambiguous strategic issues. There is chaos when managers work in groups to learn and develop new strategies—the tensions they generate through the way they interact and exercise their power produce patterns of behavior that fall into recognizable categories, but are always different in specific terms. Chaotic dynamics are evidenced by escalating small changes and self-reinforcing circles, in the manner in which managers deal with events and actions that have long-term consequences. Chaotic dynamics result from the use of both amplifying and damping feedback and produce behavioral archetypes of the kind we saw when discussing Senge's study in Chapter Two.

Having established that chaos is not merely confusion, consider now the evidence on the relationship between chaos and success. This relationship can be seen quite clearly, I believe, when we consider the nature of successful relationships between an organization and its environment and also the nature of the decision-making or control processes appropriate for conditions of great uncertainty. I will argue that in both cases managers either intentionally use both amplifying and damping feedback loops or they are unintentionally caught up in them. The result is the clearly observable escalation of small changes and the development of self-reinforcing circles with unpredictable consequences that are chaos.

Amplifying and Damping Feedback and the Environment:
Creating and Satisfying Customer Demands

Consider first the relationships between successful managers and the people who constitute the environment of their business. The stable equilibrium mind-set includes the unquestioned assumption that the requirements of customers are independent givens outside the influence of the managers responding to them. These requirements can be discovered through market research, through paying attention to communications from customers, through making trial offerings and seeing how customers respond. Once customers' needs are known, this mind-set holds, the successful company fulfills them as well as it can. If these needs change, the company will change its offerings accordingly in order to sustain adaptive equilibrium. In this view, the competitor making the best-adapted offering will be the most successful. The only form of feedback, or control, this requires is the negative or damping kind.

However, this view ignores the complex feedback nature of the relationships between managers and customers that we find in reality. Successful managers in fact create, or at least shape, the requirements of their customers through intentional and unintentional actions embodied in their product offerings. The offerings are responded to by customers, and their responses lead managers to make subsequent changes in a perpetual feedback loop.

For example, Sony created a demand for personal hi-fi systems through its Walkman offering. Atari created a demand for computer games, and Apple Computers created a demand for personal computers. Other manufacturers and operators have created a demand for portable telephones. Sony and Matsushita created the demand for video recorders. The demand for yellow "Post-It" notes was created by 3M. And so on. In these cases, managers did not simply identify what customers clearly wanted and then provide it. Rather, the managers made an offering, customers responded, the managers responded to the response, and so on through time.

This shaping activity also takes place when services rather

than goods are sold. When a management consultant and client begin to talk about a possible assignment, for example, the client does not normally have a completely clear idea of the services required from the consultant. The consultant helps to shape the client's requirements through discussion—that is, feedback. Similarly, when a representative of a company supplying information systems meets with a client, the client does not normally have a completely specified system in mind. Often, the client does not know even roughly what he or she wants. In such cases the supplier plays a considerable role in shaping the customer's requirement.

A business's offering can create or modify customer requirements, and these new requirements in turn affect subsequent offerings. This is not the one-way relationship implied by the idea of a business adapting to its environment. Instead, it is not only a feedback loop but an alternately amplifying and damping one. Creative managers seize on small differences in customer requirements and perceptions and build these into significant differentiators for their products—amplifying feedback. Then they establish quality and cost targets against which they control production of the product to satisfy the demand they have created—negative feedback. Customers may respond to this by switching from other products, leading to a virtuous circle. Alternatively, as happened several years ago with the "new" Coca-Cola, a small change in ingredients led to a massive switch away from the product, thereby creating a vicious circle until management took measures to stop it.

There are other important feedback loops, in addition to those between a firm and its customers, that determine the demand for a firm's products. For example, there is a feedback loop between the current and previous demands presented by customers. In other words, the history of customers' previous responses is incorporated into their current responses. For example, customers have fairly fixed requirements for washing machines. The more machines they buy today, the fewer they will want tomorrow (until the present machines break down). Thus, present demand feeds back into future demand.

Copying and spreading behavior on the part of customers also sets up nonlinear feedback loops. Customers often discover that they want a product when they see other people using it, and as more people use it, even more want it. This is in fact a copying and spreading feedback loop that may easily produce cumulative and self-reinforcing effects. For example, the more people buy IBM personal computers, the more software companies will produce programs for those computers. The more IBM-compatible software is available, the more attractive IBM computers will become.

W. Brian Arthur describes how copying and spreading affected the "technology war" in video cassette recorders:

> The video technology of Sony's Betamax exhibits market self-reinforcement in the sense that increased prevalence on the market encourages video outlets to stock more film titles in Betamax; there are coordination benefits to new purchasers of Betamax that increase with its market share. If Betamax and its rival VHS compete, a small lead in market share gained by one of the technologies may enhance its competitive position and help it further increase its lead. There is positive feedback. If both systems start out at the same time, market shares may fluctuate at the outset, as external circumstances and "luck" change, and as backers maneuver for advantage. And if the self-reinforcing mechanism is strong enough, eventually one of the two technologies may accumulate enough advantage to take 100% of the market. Notice however we cannot say in advance which one this will be. . . . If one technology is inherently "better" than the other . . . but has "bad luck" in gaining early adherents, the eventual outcome may not be of maximum possible benefit. (In fact, industry specialists claim that the actual loser in the video contest, Betamax, is technically superior to VHS.) . . . Once a "solution" is reached, it is difficult to exit from. In the video case, the dominant system's accrued advantage makes it difficult for the loser to break into the market again.[8]

We can clearly see that amplifying feedback leads to self-reinforcing circles that are virtuous or beneficial for some and vicious for others.

When managers intentionally shape customer demands through the offerings they make, this feeds back into customer responses, and thus profitability, each time the business moves around its profit feedback loop. Managers may increase these impacts by intentionally using the copying and spreading effects through which responses to product offerings feed back into other customers' responses and thus into the profit feedback loop. When they do this, they are deliberately using positive feedback—along with negative feedback controls to meet cost and quality targets, for example—to create business success. The successful business is also quite clearly affected by many amplifying feedback processes that are outside the control of its managers and produce effects that they did not intend. Successful businesses are quite clearly characterized by feedback processes that flip between the negative and the positive, the damping and the amplifying; that is, they are characterized by feedback patterns that produce chaos.

This becomes even clearer when we remember that customers are only part of a business's environment and that the feedback loops we have just described therefore are only some of the many in operation. A business's environment also includes competitors, suppliers, government regulators, and many others. When managers in one organization take some action, managers in other organizations respond. These responses in turn lead to further actions on the part of the first set of managers, and so on. For example, when one company cuts its prices, a competitor may respond by cutting its prices as well. The first cuts prices still further, other competitors join in, and a self-reinforcing price war ensues. Suppliers and regulatory agencies also exert a shaping influence on a company's product offerings. Feedback loops involving all these players, too, may be employed intentionally by managers, or those managers may find themselves unintentionally sucked into alternately amplifying and damping feedback processes.

Together these intended and unintended feedback loops, of both the positive and the negative kind, make it pointless to talk about a firm adapting to its environment. Managers and the people who constitute their firm's environment together create what happens through their interaction. It is not at all clear who adapts to whom. In this sense, the idea that innovative success is some form

of adaptation loses its meaning. As we begin to understand innovative success in terms of nonlinear feedback processes and
escalating circles, so we increasingly question the idea that success
and stable equilibrium can be equated. Persuasive empirical evidence that they cannot be equated is provided by the studies of
Miller and Pascale already referred to in Chapter Two. These studies show that companies fail as they move toward either stable or
unstable equilibrium states. When we consider how innovative
companies are driven by both positive and negative feedback loops,
intended and unintended, we reach the conclusion that they inevitably display chaotic behavior patterns.

Amplifying and Damping Feedback in Control Systems

The conclusion that the dynamics of success are chaotic is strength-
ened when we consider the control system of a business itself. Control systems are feedback loops in which one outcome triggers
actions that yield further outcomes. When it comes to designing
their control systems—that is, the organizational structures, information systems, management styles, and processes and procedures
of decision making—all businesses are powerfully pulled in two
fundamentally different directions, a paradox that has been recog-
nized in the management literature for a long time now. It was one
of the central conclusions of the well-known Lawrence and Lorsch
study[9] and it forms the "fit/split" basis of Pascale's model of successful companies summarized in Chapter Two. The paradox is as
follows.

On the one hand, efficiency requires task division, market
segmentation, and production process separation in geographical
and other terms. Efficiency is secured through breaking things up
into components—through some form of fragmentation. These requirements of efficiency can be met only if individuals and organizational subunits are motivated by satisfying their individual goals.
The need for efficiency thus leads to fragmenting cultures, dispersed
power, and informal channels of communication. All these factors
pull an organization and its control systems toward disintegration.
We can think of this as a form of explosively unstable equilibrium.
We can see this pull appearing in practice as companies divide

management functions in greater and greater detail, as they split the organization up into more and more decentralized business units. The more this decentralization proceeds, the harder it becomes to maintain control and hold the organization together.

To avoid this pull to disintegration and so preserve efficiency, all businesses are also pulled to a state in which tasks are integrated, overlaps in market segments and production processes are carefully controlled so that the conflicts over the overlaps are contained, group goals are stressed above individual ones, power is concentrated, communication and procedures are formalized, and strongly shared cultures are established. As a company moves in this direction, it develops more and more rigid structures, rules, procedures, and systems. Organizations that continue to develop their control systems in this direction eventually ossify. This is a very stable equilibrium position—so stable that the organization cannot cope with rapid change.

One powerful set of forces, then, pulls every business control system toward a stable equilibrium of ossification, and another powerful set pulls it toward an explosively unstable equilibrium of disintegration. Success lies between these states, in a border area where the organization continually alters aspects of its control system to avoid attraction to either disintegration or ossification. For this reason we observe all successful business organizations on what seems to be a perpetual merry-go-round between centralization and decentralization. Once again, success lies in a nonequilibrium situation between stable and unstable equilibria. For a nonlinear feedback system, that is the chaos border area. (Although not expressed in these terms, Miller and Pascale reach much the same conclusions in their studies surveyed in Chapter Two).

In control, just as in dealing with the environment, success lies in a state of bounded instability. Successful control systems combine aspects of stability and instability. They use both negative and positive feedback. Short-term control is the application of negative feedback, but managers also use amplifying feedback to handle issues with long-term consequences. When they are confronted by ambiguous issues with potentially significant but unclear long-term consequences, they form coalitions to secure attention for those issues. They use the political tools of persuasion, negotiation, and discussion to spread or amplify new ideas through the organization. A small change, in the form of a new issue dimly perceived by one or two managers, can escalate into the undertaking of a major new activity by the company. Once embarked upon, the buildup of that new activity can become either a virtuous or vicious circle.

A New Understanding of Success: Bounded Instability

The new scientific understanding of the dynamics of complex systems provides a fundamentally different mental model through which to interpret business behavior and design innovative management actions. Unlike today's most prominent mental models, it does not focus simply on stability, consistency, and cohesion as the prerequisites of business success. Because it is built upon appreciation of the continuing interactive feedback involved in the competitive game, it provides a more realistic insight into the mechanisms of that creatively unfolding game. It explicitly recognizes the unstable, disorderly aspects of the game. It accounts for the escalation of small changes and the self-reinforcing virtuous and vicious circles that the game generates. When managers design their actions with such a mental model, they will not confuse success with simple stability. They will not seek to impose the order of plans and visions upon conditions that make it impossible for those plans and visions to contribute to effective long-term control. Instead, they will seek to operate in conditions of bounded instability. They will seek to interact creatively with the other people who constitute the environment of their business.

We can now summarize the key points of this new mind-set. First, businesses are systems consisting of webs of feedback loops since every performance indicator is interconnected with every other in some way, and they are all subject to time lags. Every performance indicator therefore feeds back into a relationship that connects it to its own future values. For example, cash and profit are ploughed back into the business to yield further cash and profit flows. What happened yesterday affects what happens today, and that in turn affects what happens tomorrow. The links between performance now and performance tomorrow are provided by the decision-making process of the company and by its relationships with other organizations and individuals in its environment. Furthermore, each of these links is itself a web of feedback loops. The more responsive the decision-making process and relationships with the environment become—that is, the more sensitive the set of feedback mechanisms—the faster the business moves around the loops. These feedback mechanisms are nonlinear because their operation is constrained by capacity; finance; skills; fundamental economic laws of demand, diminishing returns, and economies of scale; and the universal tendency of people to under- and overreact to stimuli.

We have always thought that such systems have a choice between two states of behavior. They can either behave in a stable, orderly manner, which the use of negative feedback can secure, or they can operate in a much higher state of sensitivity in which feedback becomes positive, resulting in explosive instability. Both of these are equilibrium states. Since a business system obviously does not benefit from disintegration, its only hope of long-term success would appear to lie in maintaining a stable equilibrium in which it adapts to its environment. If we observe that a business develops in an unstable, irregular manner, we have to conclude— based on this mind-set—that either its managers are incompetently operating their control systems or they are subjected to random shocks from the environment to which they cannot react fast enough. This conclusion leaves us with the comforting hope that further research will reveal the list of prescriptions that will enable us to overcome our incompetence and ignorance. The comfortable land of stability is at least possible in principle.

However, scientists have discovered that a third choice is open to a nonlinear feedback system such as a business. That choice is a state of limited or bounded instability. As the sensitivity of a nonlinear feedback system is increased, it moves from stable equilibrium and passes through a phase of bounded instability before becoming explosively unstable. That phase of bounded instability has been named chaos. Chaotic behavior is random and hence unpredictable at the specific or individual level. The particular behavior that emerges is highly sensitive to small changes and therefore depends to some extent upon chance. This is not explosive instability, however, because the behavior is constrained. For this same reason, chaotic behavior always displays an irregular pattern of category features, a qualitative family resemblance. In this state of bounded instability, a system uses both positive and negative feedback autonomously.

Since a business is a system driven by nonlinear feedback loops, it must be capable of all three states of behavior. But in which of these states must a business operate if it is to be an innovative success over the long term? The answer is that it must strenuously seek to remain in the chaos area, continually resisting the strong forces pulling it toward either the equilibrium of stability or the equilibrium of instability. There are two reasons why this is so.

First, equilibrium relationships between a firm and its environment lead to failure. On the one hand, if managers give in to the feeling of security that comes from building on their strengths, the business will be pulled toward the stable equilibrium of adaptation to its environment: it does what its customers want, and it continues to do so until they signal a change. Here the business is not innovative and will succumb to its more imaginative rivals. On the other hand, there are powerful forces of complacency, shared culture, and received wisdom that pull the managers of a business toward isolation from their environment, where they ignore what the customers want and what the competitors are doing. Here, too, in this state of unstable equilibrium, a business is not innovative and will soon fall prey to its rivals. We reach the conclusion (as did Miller in the study referred to in Chapter Two) that neither equilibrium position is compatible with innovation. It follows that only the chaos border between them is: the process of creating and satisfying new demands is one of continuing feedback interaction between a business and the players in its environment that takes both amplifying and damping forms and produces the clearly observable hallmarks of chaos—small changes that escalate into self-reinforcing virtuous and vicious circles.

The second reason for equating success and chaos arises from the nature of business control systems. Here too, firms that reach equilibrium positions fail. On the one hand, there are powerful forces that pull an organization toward the stable equilibrium of integration and centralization in which, by definition, control systems operate in a negative feedback mode only. If an organization gives in to these forces, it will ossify and so be incapable of handling rapid change or innovation. On the other hand, powerful forces pull an organization toward division and differentiation, where control systems operate in an amplifying mode. The endpoint of this is the unstable equilibrium of disintegration. Successful organizations must resist the pull to both ossification and disintegration and operate, instead, in a state far from equilibrium. This is also the conclusion reached by Pascale in the study described in Chapter Two. When managers employ control systems that utilize both negative and positive feedback at the same time, they sustain their organization in a state of chaos, which makes it possible for innovation to occur.

Sustaining an organization far from equilibrium in chaos is a difficult undertaking that few will continually succeed in accomplishing. What we would expect to find is that even the most successful will be sucked periodically toward some equilibrium, where they will start to fail, before some major shakeup pushes them back into the chaos area again, where they have the potential but not the guarantee of success. As they begin to fail, the media will pronounce them "dead." Then, once they have revived, they will appear on someone's list of "excellent" companies, from which they will inevitably slip in a few years. This is not necessarily a consequence of either incompetence or ignorance—although it may be a consequence of both. It could simply be a consequence of the inherent dynamics of success.

To put the argument of this chapter into perspective, consider its relationship to the studies of Senge, Miller, and Pascale described in Chapter Two. This chapter approached the question of organizational success from a feedback systems perspective, just as Senge does. The difference is that this chapter has made the nonlinearity of those feedback processes the center of attention and brought to bear new scientific discoveries about the nature of nonlinear feedback. This emphasis on nonlinearity leads to different conclusions. While Senge concludes that cause and effect are distant from each other in complex systems and therefore difficult to trace, this chapter concludes that the linkage between cause and effect disappears and is therefore impossible to trace.

This different conclusion has extremely important consequences. It means that the future of an innovative system is absolutely unknowable. An innovative system, therefore, cannot be driven to some planned or envisioned future state—a conclusion to be explored in Chapter Six. The system's future cannot be intended by its managers; it can only emerge from the chaotic interaction between it and the systems constituting its environment. In other words, successful (that is, creative) organizations avoid equilibrium and operate in states of nonequilibrium. This conclusion links the arguments of this chapter to those of Pascale (see Chapter Two), who identifies successful companies with nonequilibrium states of contradiction and tension. The conclusion about equilibrium also links the arguments of this chapter with those of Miller (see Chapter Two), who identifies failure with states of equilibrium.

Chaos theory provides a framework to bring together the studies of Senge, Miller, and Pascale, as well as the much older thinking of Hayek, Schumpeter, and others, to be mentioned in later chapters. And chaos theory takes us forward to a much more fundamental questioning of the role of intention in human organizations, the nature of control, and what we mean by strategic thinking, all matters to be discussed in later chapters.

The conclusion we reach, then, is that managers of excellent companies seek bounded instability, even though they may not be explicitly aware of doing so, because it is vital to success. Instability is not just due to ignorance or incompetence but rather is a fundamental property of successful business systems. Successful managers use constrained instability in a positive way to provoke innovation. The next chapter explores how businesses do this—in other words, how they create order out of chaos.

4

Creativity and Continuous Chaos: Discovering the Undiscovered in Complex Organizations

The last chapter discussed how well-defined, orderly systems could generate chaotic behavior. It concluded that a successful business organization is one that operates in chaos. This chapter considers other scientific discoveries about the behavior of dynamic systems that shed light on how such systems produce new order from chaos. It describes the relationship between chaos and the process of creativity.

Symmetry Breaking: How Chaos Leads to Creativity

In today's rapidly changing environment, businesses must continually create and innovate to succeed. But when systems are close to adaptive equilibrium, they require major internal changes in order to be creative or even to cope with major random shocks from the environment. This means that innovation is very hard for a business in stable equilibrium. Doing new things requires altering stable relationships between people, work patterns, attitudes, perceptions, and cultures.

When a system operates far from equilibrium, however, its behavior can be changed much more easily. We saw in Chapter Three that when a company operates in chaos, perceptions, attitudes, and cultures are not strongly shared. Managers do not try to control the long-term development of their business according to rules, objectives, and plans. Instead they engage in political interaction to expose ambiguous and contentious issues. They use conflict and dialogue to clarify and progress those issues. The bounded instability of contention makes the positive contribution of shattering old perceptions and attitudes and preventing rigid, uniform cultures from developing. In these conditions, small changes can easily escalate into major changes of behavior.

In the language of the scientists, chaos breaks symmetries, and this is an essential step in the emergence of new order. Destruction and creativity are closely related to each other, and continuing creativity requires continuing destruction. This is by no means a new idea in economics or business. Back in the 1930s, the economist Schumpeter[1] stressed that a firm must practice "creative destruction" on itself if it wants to sustain competitive advantage. It must destroy its old advantages by creating new ones; if it does not, some rival will.

New discoveries—the theory of self-organization[2]—about the way nonlinear feedback systems develop new order out of chaos in nature add greatly to these old ideas. Take modern explanations for the laser beam. At a low temperature, a gas may be very close to thermodynamic equilibrium, in which the atoms behave in a particular way and emit hardly any light. If the system is driven away from equilibrium by heating the gas, the atoms enter excited states, with each atom emitting light randomly and independently. The light from the atoms emerges as an incoherent jumble of light waves, and as a result, the gas behaves like an ordinary lamp, with its light extending over only a few meters. The behavior of the atoms has become chaotic, with atoms pointing in many different directions, and the effect of this chaos has been to break the behavior pattern that the gas exhibited when cold. It is as if the chaos is freeing the system up to do something new. During this chaos, as heat continues to be pumped into the gas, a critical point is reached, and the atoms suddenly organize themselves on a global scale to display cooperative behavior of a very precise kind. At the same instant, each atom aligns itself with all the others, as if they are communicating and cooperating throughout the gas, so that they all point in precisely the same direction. This means that all the atoms emit waves of light that are exactly in phase. The result is a coherent ray of light—laser light—stretching over very long distances. Ordinary light is like a water sprinkler; laser light is like a fire hose. The phenomenon of laser light is not predictable from the laws of physics; that is, there is nothing in the normal laws of physics to predict that this will happen or to explain why it happens.[3] The laser is not a new equilibrium state of behavior for the gas. It is a far-from-equilibrium state, one scientists call a "dissipative structure" because it dissipates energy and will continue to exist only while heat is pumped into the system to replace that dissipated energy.

Another example of spontaneous self-organization in a system driven far from equilibrium occurs when a horizontal layer of fluid is heated from below. The warm liquid at the bottom rises. At low temperatures the warm fluid rises to the top in an orderly manner. But when the temperature is raised further, the liquid becomes unstable and starts to convect. When the temperature at the bottom of the layer of fluid reaches a critical point, the convecting liquid suddenly adopts a highly orderly and stable pattern, organizing itself into distinctive rolls with a hexagonal cell structure. The detailed arrangement of the convection cells cannot be predicted, and the experimenter has no control over whether a given part of the fluid will end up in a clockwise or counterclockwise rotating cell.

The theory of self-organization is a revolutionary new way of understanding how natural systems work. For centuries, scientists have worked on the assumption that all natural systems tend to equilibrium, where they operate according to a predetermined design that is fixed for all time—the cosmic vision and the cosmic plan. Change was always thought of as a move from one equilibrium state to another. With this model of the world, scientists always had difficulty explaining phase transitions (water turning to steam, for example) and turbulence in gasses and liquids. Now, however, scientists work with models in which natural systems always operate away from equilibrium and change in unpredictable ways to create their own futures. The Nobel prize–winning chemist, Illya Prigogine, claims that most systems in nature operate far from equilibrium.

To summarize, scientists have discovered that when nonlinear feedback systems are pushed far from equilibrium, they follow a common sequence of steps in which they may move from one state, through chaos, to unpredictable states of new order. These new states of order are not comfortable equilibrium ones in which the system easily stays until disturbed again but dissipative structures that are difficult to sustain because they require continual inputs of energy if they are to survive. The common sequence of steps is as follows. At each point of transition, systems driven far from equilibrium move through patterns of instability in which previous symmetry or order is broken, thus confronting the system with choices at critical points. Through a process of spontaneous self-organization, a form of communication and cooperation among the components of the system, new order may be produced. Such phase transitions do not necessarily have predictable outcomes; the possibility is there in some cases for the system to make choices that produce new and unexpected behavior. Chance may be involved in moving from one state to another. This is definitely not a possibility in or near to equilibrium states, where outcomes are predictable.

In chaos then, creativity is a potentially ongoing process that is internally generated in a spontaneous manner. It is neither proaction according to some prior design nor reaction to environmental change, but rather continuing interaction with other systems in the environment. A system in this state creates its own environment and its own future.

We can observe exactly the same process as that just described for natural systems when managers in a successful business handle open-ended strategic issues. Their strategic management is a process of symmetry-breaking instability and destruction that generates new perspectives, sudden consensus at critical points, and spontaneous self-organization that can produce the order of innovation and new strategic direction out of chaos.

Some managers are startled at first by the idea that instability plays a vitally important role in continuing creativity and that innovations arise unpredictably from some kind of centrally uncontrolled, spontaneous process. But the idea is not really that startling. Managers frequently reorganize the structures of their companies, using the following justification: "This reorganization will change relationships between people; it will alter work patterns; and it will convey strong messages that things are going to be different." Such reorganizations are purposely destabilizing and have the explicit intention of shattering existing patterns of attitudes, personal relationships, and work. They use instability to bring about change. These procedures quite clearly imply some reliance on self-organization, for if the new organization could set out quite unambiguously what people were now to do and ensure that they did it, there would be no need to talk about changing attitudes and relationships or sending messages. The aim of these reorganizations is to create conditions in which people will spontaneously do things differently. Managers may introduce other destabilizing changes for the same purpose.

Evidence that some managers intentionally provoke instability in order to alter behavior patterns and encourage spontaneous creativity is provided by a study carried out by Ikujiro Nonaka.[4] His survey of Japanese companies shows how they use chaos for self-renewal. Consider some quotes:

> Honda is well known for a culture in which confrontation is encouraged among employees regardless of rank. Kawashima, the former president, has been quoted as saying, "I decided to step down as president because the employees began agreeing with me 70 percent of the time."

> Countercultures are formed by hiring new employees with diverse specialities and introducing new employees through mid-career employment. The Copier Division of Canon Inc., for example, has many employees who joined the company through mid-way hiring. It is necessary to keep hiring these people until a certain critical mass is reached so that they will be able to oppose the existing values. At Honda, mid-way hiring is practised in order to "give impact to existing persons and organization through the introduction of new blood." Moreover, it is customarily done deliberately every two or three years instead of employing a fixed number each year.

Canon's President Kaku says, "A company begins to decline as soon as one thinks it has become a premier company. There are two things which the top management must keep in mind in order to guarantee the continuing existence of the company. The first task of top management is to create a vision that gives meaning to the employees' jobs. The second task is to constantly convey a sense of crisis to their employees."

There is other evidence that firms go through phases very similar to the self-organizing stages displayed by nonlinear feedback systems in nature. Phases of this kind have been demonstrated in the relatively few studies so far made of political processes in business organizations.[5] According to these studies, some change or galvanizing event provokes conflict concerning the way it should be handled. Different individuals or organizational subunits become champions of different options. Each champion forms a coalition of others who have something to gain from that option, thus building political support for it. The option chosen depends upon which coalition has the greatest power. Politics and the use of power overcome the initial conflict, and once an option is agreed upon, all work together to implement it.

In these explanations, conflict plays a part in the selection of options to be considered, but the role of functional political activity is seen as being to resolve that conflict and restore consensus as quickly as possible. The normal state for the organization is pictured as consensus and commitment. Functional politics in this view is a negative feedback, damping form of control that sustains cohesion and harmony. Any other form of politics is said to be dysfunctional. Politics here is seen as the temporary instability between one equilibrium state and another.

The process of change in an organization is also usually described in terms of a phase of unfreezing, followed by a phase of reformulating, followed in turn by a phase of refreezing. A popular scheme for explaining group behavior in organizations is that of phases in which groups form, storm, norm, and then perform. Here too there is the idea that change involves temporary bouts of instability as organizations and groups move from the safety of one state of equilibrium to another.

These ideas about politics and change in human organizations are close to the descriptions given earlier of the self-organizing phases of systems in nature. An understanding of the chaotic and self-organizing dynamics of nonlinear systems, however, leads to a rather different perspective on the role of organizational politics. From this perspective, politics is an amplifying feedback loop whose purpose is to encourage conflict and spread questioning attitudes. Functional politics then involves continual dialogue around contentious issues. It is the mechanism for attracting organizational attention to open-ended issues. Its function is to spread instability, within boundaries. Such instability is necessary to shatter existing patterns of behavior and perceptions so that the new may emerge. Conflict, dissent, and lack of commitment are the norm in continually innovating organizations. Only at critical points do commitment and consensus concerning some particular issue appear, and they soon dissipate when the next contentious issue arises. Political activity and the learning associated with it are essentially self-organizing, and it is the process through which the order of new strategic direction emerges.

The dynamic systems interpretation of political activity in a business focuses attention on political instability as a continuing condition of creativity rather than a temporary misfortune between one stable state and another. In the rest of this chapter we consider the sense in which businesses follow the same phases as other nonlinear feedback systems as they change.

Seven Phases in Managing Strategic Issues

If we observe how managers actually behave when confronted by open-ended changes, we will see that there is a rhythm to, or a number of phases in, that behavior. These seven phases are depicted in Figure 4.1.

The behavior depicted in Figure 4.1 is the discovering, choosing, and acting that constitutes organizational learning and political interaction. Let us examine each phase in that behavior separately.

Figure 4.1. Managing Strategic Issues.

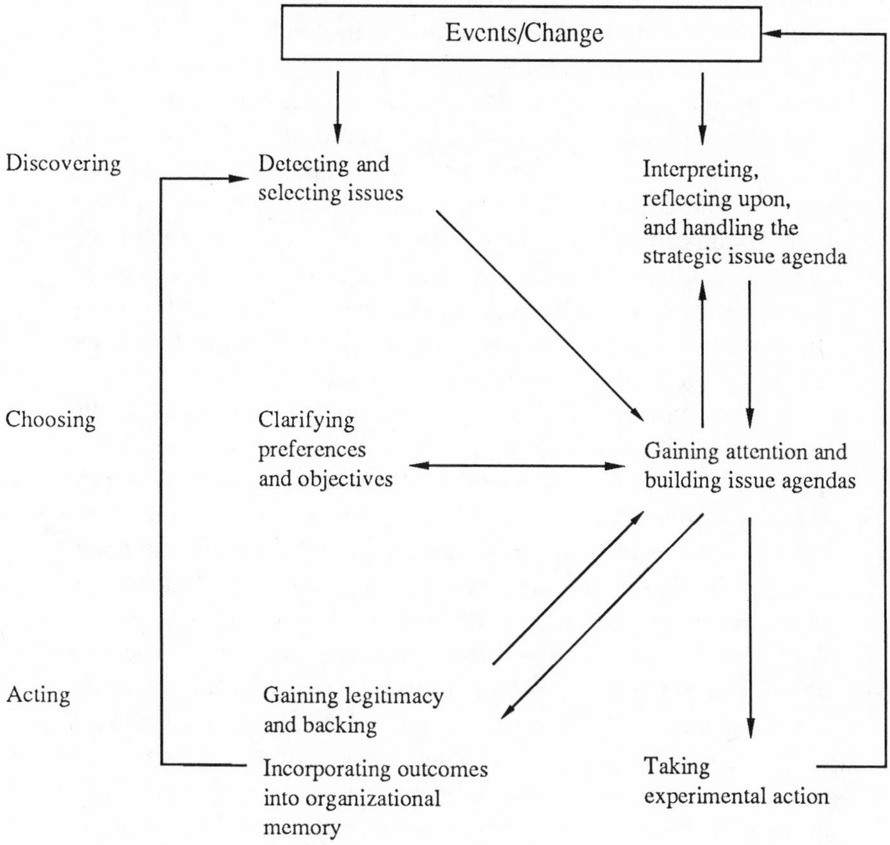

Detecting and Selecting Issues

Open-ended change—the kind that strategic management is concerned with—is typically the result of many accumulated small events and actions. Such change is unclear, ambiguous, and confusing, with consequences that are unknowable. The key difficulty for managers is to identify the real issues, problems, and opportunities involved in the change and then find an appropriate response in the form of a creative aspiration or objective. The first step in conventional strategic management prescriptions is the setting of an or-

ganizational objective. But how does a group of managers do this
when they rightly feel equivocal and conflict with each other in
ambiguous and unpredictable situations? In these circumstances the
organization has no alternative but to rely on the initiative of individuals to notice and pursue some issue, aspiration, or challenge,
as an individual, not as a group or an organization. In order to do
this, those individuals in turn have to rely on their experience-based
intuition and ability to detect analogies between one set of ambiguous circumstances and another. These activities are spontaneous
and self-organizing in the sense that no central authority can direct
anyone to detect and select a particular open-ended issue for attention, simply because no one knows what that issue is until someone
has detected it. You cannot instruct someone to have a good idea.

The importance of this reliance on the spontaneous, self-
organizing ability of individuals intuitively to detect and select
open-ended issues is most obvious in the case of well-known individual entrepreneurs. For example, the history of Amstrad, from its
founding in the 1970s to the present time, is a story of the open-
ended issues that its founder, Alan Sugar, detected and selected for
attention. He noticed in the 1970s that plastic covers for record
players would be much cheaper if they were made by an injection
molding rather than a vacuum forming process. This led to the
creation of a lucrative product. He detected that most people did not
want to go to the trouble of assembling a number of different hi-
fi units, but they nonetheless liked the fashionable appearance of a
multiunit hi-fi set. So he created tower systems that consisted of one
unit but looked like a number of different units. Sales of these low-
priced all-in-one units ran into millions. Sugar then detected that
potential customers for personal computers knew too little about
such systems to be able to assemble a number of different units and
load software onto them. So he created a low-cost product that could
be taken from the store, plugged in, and used immediately. This
happens in other companies, too. Recall the example in Chapter
One of Ukita, who detected the Discman in a failed CD player.

Gaining Attention and Building Issue Agendas

The birth of a strategy is no different in any other corporation. Some
individual, at some level in the hierarchy, detects some potential

issue and begins to push for organizational attention to be paid to that issue. What does differ between an organization run by an all-powerful entrepreneur and others is the complexity of the political process required to gain attention for an issue. At Amstrad an issue received organizational attention if—and only if—Alan Sugar was persuaded to attend to it. In most organizations, however, a more complex process of building special-interest groups or coalitions around an issue is required before that issue can be said to have gained organizational attention. This political activity of building support for attention to some detected issue is also clearly self-organizing and spontaneous in the sense that it is informal and not part of normal rules and procedures. No one is centrally organizing the factions and coalitions that form around detected issues.

Interpeting, Reflecting upon, and Handling the Strategic Issue Agenda

Once the demand to pay attention to an issue has gained sufficient support, in the sense that it is being discussed by those with sufficient power to do something about it, that issue becomes part of the organization's strategic issue agenda. This agenda is at the heart of strategic management. It is the focus of the organizational learning through which a business develops new strategic directions. The strategic agenda is an unwritten list of all the issues, aspirations, and challenges to which key groups of managers are attending. The agenda is dynamic, constantly changing in a manner that reflects what is being detected, how the pattern of political interplay is developing, and what managers are learning. Issues arrive on the agenda. Some are attended to. Others drop off the list without ever being acted upon. Still others are successfully enacted, while others lead to actions that fail. Successful companies—creative companies—have live, active strategic issue agendas. At Amstrad in the mid-1980s, for example, the agenda contained large numbers of issues related to different computer products, finding sources of components in the Far East, manufacturing and assembly, setting up distribution channels in Europe, organizational structures and control systems, and so on.

When managers deal with the issues on their strategic agenda, they are learning as they go. There is no overall framework to which they can refer before they decide how to tackle an issue because strategic issues are unique, ambiguous, and ill structured. Through discussion with each other and with customers, suppliers, and competitors they discover what objectives they should pursue and what actions might work. They alter old mental models, existing company and industry recipes, to come up with new ways of doing things. They discover and clarify preferences, aspirations, and goals.

The communication that all of this involves is spontaneous in the sense that it is not directed by a central authority. It depends upon individuals and thus upon the boundary conditions or context provided by individual personalities, the dynamics of their interaction with each other, and the time they have available given all the other issues that require attention.

When managers deal with the strategic issue agenda of their organization, they are performing a vitally important destabilizing function. Strategic issues, by definition, threaten existing work patterns, organizational structures, and power positions. Strategic issues are about new, different ways of doing things and different things to do. Carrying issues through discussion, conflict, and dialogue changes perceptions. This instability and confusion, or chaos, performs the function of shattering the existing order—the system's symmetry—to make the new possible. Handling issues on the agenda, building support for various courses of action, amplifies this instability through the system.

Clarifying Preferences and Objectives

Some issues on an organization's agenda may be dealt with very quickly. Others may attract attention (continuous or periodic) for a very long time. How quickly an issue is dealt with depends upon the time required to reach enough consensus and commitment to proceed to action. It thus depends upon the course that the political and learning interaction takes. At some critical point, some external pressure, or some internal pressure arising from power, personality, or group interaction, in effect forces a choice. The outcome—the decision about what, if any, action to take regarding an issue—is unpredictable because it depends upon the context of power, personality, and group dynamics.

The consensus required to proceed to action is temporary, fragile, and related only to a specific issue. When the group of managers turns to the next issue, consensus must be established anew. In a dynamic organization—one dealing with an active, ever-changing issue agenda—consensus is the exception, not the norm. Sustaining consensus requires continuing inputs of energy and attention. Consensus in such an organization is what scientists call a dissipative structure because it tends to dissipate unless energy is constantly fed in to maintain it.

Taking Experimental Action

Action will usually be experimental at first, thus providing a vehicle for further learning. For example, Amstrad first set up agents in France, Spain, and Germany. Once this limited distribution demonstrated realizable potential, subsidiary companies were established in these countries.

Actors in the environment respond to the actions that managers in a company take. Through their responses, those environmental actors change the situation. Such changes are fed back into the learning loop of the company and lead to further learning and thus to further action. (The Amstrad operations in France, Spain, and Germany all developed in different ways, and Amstrad learned from them. It used the French model, which proved to be the most successful, to redesign operations in Spain and Germany.) Task forces may be set up to carry out experimental actions such as the development of a new product. The operation of such task forces is a continuing political and learning process.

Gaining Legitimacy and Backing

Building and handling strategic issue agendas proceeds largely outside the formal structures and procedures of an organization. Such bodies merely provide the boundaries within which this self-organizing process occurs. Nonetheless, at various points in the process, often before experimental action is taken and certainly before such action is built into a strategy, formal bodies and procedures are required to legitimize the choices being made and to allocate resources to the exploration of or experimentation with issues. These bodies become important mainly after unclear, open-ended issues have proceeded through learning and experimentation and are ready to emerge as potentially successful new strategies. New strategies can be carried out only if those powerful bodies back them with sufficient resources. The support and interest of the formal bodies in an organization thus is vital to the effective building and handling of strategic issues, even though such bodies are essentially peripheral to the process.

Incorporating Outcomes into Organizational Memory

Managers in a business come to share memories of what has worked or failed to work in the past. In this way they build up a business philosophy for their company; they establish a company recipe. In common with their competitors, they build industry recipes as well. These recipes, taken together, become the culture or organizational memory. This is often referred to as a "vision," even though it is really retrospective rather than prospective. After action has been taken on a strategic issue, the successful or unsuccessful results of this action become part of the organization's memory.

An organization's memory has a powerful effect on what issues its managers will detect and attend to. It constitutes the frame of reference within which those managers interpret what to do next. This organizational memory provides yet another boundary around the instability of the political and learning processes through which strategic issues are handled. It is a boundary that has to be watched, however, because it can easily become inappropriate to new circumstances. An essential part of the complex learning process required to handle strategic issues is the continual questioning of the organization's cultural or collective memory.

For example, shortly after a speech in which Alan Sugar set out the Amstrad business philosophy of aggressive entrepreneurialism, he actually adopted a rather different approach. As David Thomas wrote, "Ironically, Sugar delivered his City University speech just as Amstrad was in the process of abandoning crucial ingredients of its ultra-entrepreneurial, small business ethos. Few people realized it at the time, but in many ways the address set the seal on the first twenty years of Amstrad's existence. Indeed, Sugar had already sown some of the seeds which would grow into structures more appropriate for a large company."[6] Successful managers do not cling blindly to one business philosophy all their lives. They learn and change their mind-set to generate new ways of doing things.

The Life Cycle of an Issue

As the foregoing has indicated, any one issue on a firm's strategic agenda has something of a life cycle. The issue starts life as a vague, half-formed idea. At this point, managers' principle tasks are to clarify it and build support for the idea of paying attention to it. Planning-related forms of control and development have no contribution to make here. But if work on that issue continues, the issue eventually reaches a stage of clarity at which objectives can be formed. Now planning enters as a way to control project execution. If at this point the outcomes of actions taken to deal with the issue are predictable, a fuller form of planning becomes possible for that project.

Issues, the consensus required to do something about them, and the objectives to achieve in regard to them all emerge from ongoing learning. Once the issues have emerged and have been clarified, other forms of control and development have a part to play. But this is planning around a major issue, not planning the future of the system as a whole.

The central part of the learning/political control and development feedback loop just described is the strategic issue agenda. This agenda is always changing. At any one time it will contain some vague issues around which intentions are many and half formed, as well as other issues that have reached an advanced stage of clarification. Still other issues will be in an intermediate stage, in which consensus and shared intention exist but no definite decisions have been made.

The feedback loop through which strategic issues are

handled operates in an amplifying manner within boundaries. It is driven by political interaction and learning in real time. It is a form of control, because behavior within it is connected and constrained. Outcomes emerge as the result of converging and emerging individual and subunit intentions.

All of the steps in this loop have been identified individually by one piece of research or another. But when we look at them from the perspective of system dynamics, we are led to focus on two important features: the positive role of instability and unpredictability, and the nature and importance of spontaneous self-organization.

Using Instability in Strategic Management

At the most visible level, that is, in the day-to-day conduct of their existing business, successful organizations display a stable, orderly face to their customers, competitors, suppliers, managers, and employees. They deliver consistent quality, on time, at cost targets. The outside world sees an understandable organizational structure focused on market segments; customers and suppliers know who they are dealing with. Those within the organization see well-defined jobs within a clear hierarchy that sets out reporting lines and responsibilities for the delivery of competitive products. They see orderly information and control systems yielding plans and targets that enable people to know what they are doing on a day-to-day basis. They are aware of their company's business philosophy, the recipe, or shared culture, built upon previous experience of successfully working together. At this visible level, success is cohesion, harmony, regularity, and order.

But a successful business operates on more than one level. In addition to applying stable, damping control to their existing business, successful organizations at the same time continually create new strategic directions. They repackage existing products and create new market segments. They identify new groups of customers, new distribution channels, new sources of supply, new approaches to manufacturing. They develop new products, new technologies, different forms of day-to-day control, different reward systems, new approaches to staff selection, new techniques for training and development. And operating at this level, where the new is created, involves behavior that is diametrically opposed to the orderly conduct of day-to-day business, because creating the new inevitably destroys the old. Almost every potential alteration in the nature or conduct of a business creates opportunities for some individuals or subunits and threatens the existing work patterns, roles, positions, or power of others. Operating at the frontiers of the new is therefore inherently destabilizing to the organization.

Furthermore, the new can arise only in conditions of instability. The heart of creative strategic management lies in the ability of managers within an organization continually to develop live, active strategic issue agendas. Strategic issues are perceived only when individuals notice some incongruity in what is currently going on—when they question the established recipes, culture, or business philosophy. Maintaining a live strategic issue agenda therefore depends upon people having different perceptions and then amplifying those perceptions throughout the organization by means of political activity. Multiple perceptions thrive when cultures are not strongly shared.

Amplifying political activity is destabilizing and is unavoidably bound up with personal career concerns. It becomes difficult to distinguish between functional politics and dysfunctional politics; in practice, in fact, one cannot separate the two. Activity around the strategic issue agenda therefore inevitably is highly political. Initially, any potentially new line of development involves conflict, as well as a lack of widespread consensus and commitment. In a thriving company there are always potentially new lines of development, so there is always conflict and a lack of consensus and commitment around some issue. These are the norms for creative strategic management.

The important point is that, far from being harmful, the instability of multiple cultures and conflict around issues and careers, as well as lack of cohesion, consensus, and commitment, is vital to the continual provocation of new perceptions and ideas. In a successful organization this instability is bounded, not explosive. The boundaries are provided by clear hierarchies, unequally distributed power, different cultures, and the existing business philosophy. Creative strategic management involves continually testing these boundaries. Innovation flows from the creative tension between having boundaries and testing them.

Success, then, arises essentially out of a creative tension between the visible stability required to pursue an existing business efficiently and the far less visible bounded instability, or chaos, required to provoke creative handling of a dynamic strategic issue agenda. The tension is between the practice of negative, damping forms of control in short-term situations that involve limited change and the simultaneous practice of amplifying forms of control in long-term situations that involve open-ended change. Managers of successful companies must be able to operate in formal modes according to stable plans at one moment and then switch to informal, unstable political learning activities at the next.

Using Spontaneous Self-Organization in Strategic Management

It is impossible for those in positions of power to predetermine what open-ended changes will be detected and selected for organizational attention. This is because such changes tend to be small, and they escalate in ways that depend upon the details of what the organization and its rivals do. No central authority can predetermine or direct the course of the political activity, the formation of special interest groups and coalitions, that is necessary for the amplification of some detected change through the organization. The successful organization therefore must rely on the spontaneous self-organization of groups of managers to detect and select strategic issues for the organization's agenda.

We can see that this is what actually happens if we consider the difference between formal and informal managerial meetings. Formal board and top executive meetings are institutionalized communication arenas that perform a number of functions. They compare past results against budgets and annual plans, seeking to explain past success and failure; they legitimize proposals for action and resource allocation; they perform symbolic functions of approving plans and targets for the existing business as well as proposals to explore potential new activities; they attend to administrative matters. All these functions follow from the central purpose of the meetings, which is to oversee and legitimize the operation of the firm's hierarchical control systems and procedures. Indeed, the more efficient the company, the more effective its rules and procedures in delegating authority in predetermined circumstances, the more time top teams will find that they spend on these functions.

Typically, these functions take up the bulk of the time available at such meetings, thus crowding out what most top executives see as their prime role: that of dealing with important strategic issues. This is not surprising because the group dynamics of conformity and dependence that are provoked by the formal exercise of authority are not conducive to free-ranging discussion of strategic issues.

Strategic issues are actually dealt with at other meetings that occur spontaneously or are conducted in very informal ways. The group dynamics of these occasions are very different, more conducive to open discussion and learning. Power in the shape of formal authority is not much in evidence. Instead, we find people expressing power through influence. The outcomes of these meetings, unlike those of the formal ones, will not be predictable because small changes in behavioral dynamics can escalate to have important consequences. The most useful role of the formal meetings is to legitimize what emerges from the informal ones.

These informal strategy meetings embody not anarchy or explosive instability but bounded instability. Their boundaries are provided by the need to gain support and not be out on a limb, the existence of hierarchy and power structure, different cultures, and the dynamics of group behavior. Self-organization is not formalized widespread participation or power redistribution. Rather, it is key groups of managers who spontaneously find it worthwhile to become involved in areas outside their formal responsibility because they see those areas as important. The less this kind of spontaneous activity is confined to the top level of management, the more likely an organization is to develop new strategic directions.

Building and dealing with strategic issue agendas is a spontaneous, self-organizing process that occurs in conditions of bounded instability. It is a political and learning process. It is managers reflecting on and discussing strategic issues informally in groups. It has unpredictable outcomes, because creativity and un-predictability are closely bound together.

Handling Strategic Issues Creatively

The discovery that order can produce chaos and chaos can lead to new order should lead managers to think and act differently when considering how to develop and control a business. It directly challenges many unquestioned assumptions that most managers make about this task. On the basis of the old assumptions we design our actions by starting with some future state, either a predicted one or a desired one. We identify the gap between where we are now, or would be without changing what we do, and this future. Then we work back to see what we need to do in order to get from here to there. We try to plan or envision what we are going to do before changes happen. We gather information, we do research, we analyze options. We set up detailed rules and procedures ahead of time, using step-by-step analytical reasoning. We focus explicit attention on achieving order, harmony, and consistency, and we design over-all frameworks and blueprints to sustain that order as we move through time. And when we succeed in doing all this, we simply repeat what we have done before—and so in the end we fail.

In fact, as preceding chapters have shown, successful businesses behave quite differently, often without fully understanding what they are doing. They act in a manner that is more consistent with the chaotic view I have been presenting. If we act on the assumptions underlying this view, we design actions starting from the here and now, with challenging aspirations and ambitions, determination and initiative. We go forward from where we are, without trying to work out in advance what will happen. We use intuition, reasoning by analogy, and reflection upon experience to design innovative and creative actions to deal with present issues that we know will have important long-term consequences, even though we cannot say what those consequences will be. We act and then wait to see what happens, dealing with the consequences as they occur. In short, we learn in real time. We become very concerned with how we are learning as teams of managers, the nature of our political interaction and the effects this has on our group dynamics, and the impact of personality on learning and deciding. We become concerned not with adapting to a given, unalterable external world but with making that world what we want it to be. Proaction and reaction are replaced by continually creative interaction. We try to create conditions under which people can learn and act spontaneously, using their own initiative.

When we recognize that the future is unknowable and abandon any attempt to design our actions based on forecasts of that future, we do not abandon all concern with the long term. Instead we realize that we must continually discover, learn about, and create our long-term future. By focusing our concern on present issues that have long-term consequences, we actually deal with the long term in a more realistic and creative way. The next chapter explores what all this means for the nature of strategic thinking and learning.

5

Strategic Thinking and Continuous Contention: Confronting an Open-ended Future

The idea that order can produce chaos and chaos can produce order in creative dynamic systems is a powerful new scientific insight. It has important implications for understanding the nature of strategic thinking in a business. The new perspective forces us to confront the open-ended nature of the future of any business. Humans facing unpredictable, open-ended futures find it impossible to sustain consensus among themselves for other than short time periods around individual issues, unless they substantially suspend their critical faculties. Their prime difficulty is in framing and sharing perceptions of problems and opportunities, not in solving problems.

Effective strategic thinking in these circumstances therefore must be based on assumptions of unpredictability, weak cause-and-effect links, irregular patterns, ill-structured problems and opportunities, and continuing contention. Managers must develop new mental models for each new situation. This approach differs from commonly accepted views of strategic thinking, which focus on problem solving, predictability, close cause-and-effect links, regular patterns, and continuing harmony and consensus.

Once managers understand that a successful business is a dynamic nonlinear feedback system operating in the chaos border area, they must see strategic thinking as involving the following mental tasks:

- Developing a new mental model for each new situation rather than applying the same general prescriptions to many situations

- Anchoring one's thinking to the here and now, not the future
- Reasoning by analogy and intuition about qualitative, irregular patterns rather than analysis and quantification
- Thinking in terms of a whole, interconnected system rather than separate parts
- Focusing on the learning process, and on the mental models governing the process, rather than on outcomes
- Becoming aware of the effects of group dynamics on thinking and learning, and trying to minimize dysfunctional group dynamics

Each of these significant changes in understanding what strategic thinking means will be discussed in this chapter.

Using and Sharing Mental Models

The ability of humans to assess a situation and design a response to it is limited by the capacity of the short-term working memory of the brain. Tests have shown that we are capable of retaining and processing only up to about seven bits of information at any one time.[1] A bit may be a digit, a letter of the alphabet, or some combination of digits or letters such as a word. Long-term memory seems to have an infinite capacity, but it takes seconds to store new material in that memory. Therefore, our ability to process new information and bring to bear already stored information and techniques is severely limited.

As a result, we cope with the mass of information that constitutes reality by in effect ignoring most of it. We select only what we regard to be the most important features and relationships of whatever we observe. We construct simplified mental models of reality because this is the only way we can comprehend it and design actions to deal with it. We build up large numbers of such models in our memories, based on past experience and education, and then use them to simplify any new situations we encounter and design actions to respond to them. Our mental models constitute a frame of reference within which we think, explain, learn, prescribe, and act.

As a way to overcome further our limited brain capacities, we automate a great many of our mental models by pushing them below the level of awareness. We then call upon them automatically, without thinking about them or examining them, as soon as we recognize features of a situation to which they appear to apply. Thus an expert physician notes certain symptoms, instantly calls up an appropriate mental model, and uses it to prescribe a treatment. All experts do the same thing: they recognize key features of a category and then automatically call up an appropriate model to use in choosing their responses. (Computerized "expert systems," in fact, are designed to mimic this very process.) They do not have to sift consciously through all the models in their brains to select a response.

This is an efficient way of overcoming the limitations of the brain, but it has a serious drawback. It means that we do not question the assumptions behind a mental model before we use it. The more automatic and faster, that is the more skilled, our behavior, the less we question the mental models driving it.

When times are turbulent, this failure to question may well become an omission of great importance. Models that have worked in previous situations may not work in the new ones created by rapid change. Coping with open-ended futures and turbulent change requires continual questioning and changing of submerged mental models. Without it there is the very real possibility of what has been called skilled incompetence.[2] The behavior is skilled because it is easy, even automatic; it is incompetent because it is inappropriate to the new situation and produces unintended, undesirable outcomes.

When we work in groups, we often share our mental models. When we come to share the same implicit models, we usually accept unquestioningly the even more hidden assumptions behind them. Doing so cuts down on the time needed to exchange information and beliefs before we act together. As with an individual, however, the drawback is that we mutually reinforce each other's models and assumptions when this may not be appropriate. It means that groups of managers, just like individuals, may display a high degree of skilled incompetence when faced with rapidly changing conditions.

Can the Human Mind Cope with Chaos?

Some people reject the claim that the dynamics of successful companies are chaotic because they feel that human beings cannot cope with chaos. This response would clearly be justified if we took the limited view that humans recognize events and shapes strictly according to rigidly defined features. In this limited view, we put an item into a particular category if, and only if, the item has all the defining features of the category. A category is seen as clear cut, containing individuals that are in all important respects the same. We retain those clear category features in our memories, storing them much as computers do, and, when confronted with another situation, we recall those features and so know how to categorize some new phenomenon. Using these recalled features as a checklist, we apply step-by-step rules to the individual items observed in order to determine how to act in relation to them. According to this view, the process of learning would consist simply of memorizing clear-cut bodies of knowledge and formulating explicit rules, relating causes to effects, that can be applied to new situations. If this really is how human beings perceive, memorize, learn, and design actions, we would indeed have severe difficulties in dealing with items that are related to each other only through a fuzzy kind of family resemblance.

But common sense and evidence show that this is not the only, nor even the most important, way in which we classify new stimuli. Numerous tests have indicated that our memories do not store information in units representing the precise characteristics of the individual units (shapes, events, or whatever) that we perceive. Rather, we store information about the strength of connection between the units. We lump information together into categories or concepts on the basis of family resemblance-type features. We relate new information to old using typical or prototype individual events as a guide to categorization. We store in terms of relatedness or associative strength. Memory, then, emphasizes general structural content rather than specific content. Furthermore, we retain memories for exceptions. We remember in terms of deviations from the mental models we have stored as well as in terms of matches. We memorize the irregularities in the patterns we observe.

We use previously stored schemas, frames, or scenes to fill in the details of what we observe. We notice analogies between one situation and another, even when the details of the situations are quite different.[3] We are capable of spontaneously generalizing, and we are stimulated to new perspectives by paradoxes, anomalies, contradictions, and conflicts. When we confront new situations, we build new mental models by forming analogies with previous ones. The use of analogy in perceiving, classifying, and developing new mental models appears to be of great importance in human thinking. As Gick and Holyoak say, "Analogy pervades thought. . . . To make the novel seem familiar by relating it to prior knowledge, to make the familiar seem strange by viewing it from a new perspective—these are fundamental aspects of human intelligence that depend on the ability to reason by analogy. This ability is used to construct new scientific models, to design experiments, to solve new problems in terms of old ones, to make predictions, to control experiments, to construct arguments, and to interpret literary metaphors."[4]

We do not design actions in totally new situations by using step-by-step rules in which causes are clearly related to effects. Rather, we use intuition and analogies drawn from past experience, upon which we reflect and which we then adapt to suit the new situation. Differences, exceptions, and deviations from the expected play an important part in how we classify and respond to the new.

If we think of human learning and memory in this manner, we can see that chaotic situations present no real problem. In fact, we might even say that the human mind is ideally suited to handling such situations. Since in chaotic systems the individual events are always different, there is no point in storing detailed information about individual events. What we store instead, and subsequently use to design our actions, is the fuzzy family resemblances that accompany all the individual differences. In learning we use processes of reasoning by analogy, of intuition, and of reflecting on experience and adapting it to new situations, all of which are ideally suited to handling chaos. Dawkins writes in *The Blind Watchmaker:*

> Evolution has come up with two broad strategies for
> solving the problem of allowing complex behaviour.
> One is to pre-program the organism so that everything

that is necessary for efficient functioning is built into
the genes of the organism, with a minimum modification if necessary. This occurs in the case of many in-
sects and so-called "lower organisms." While such a
solution is very rigid, organisms adopting it have been
successful for far longer than man has been on the
planet, and may well outlive him by a similar margin.
The other strategy is to produce an organism which
can learn, that is one that can modify behavior to suit
the demands of the environment. The human race is
clearly the organism that is most dependent on learning and most flexible in its programming.[5]

Managers of businesses—complex systems in a complex environment—obviously need to depend on the strategy of learning.

Strategic Thinking: Analytical or Analogical?

Designing actions on the basis of new learning is much more difficult than simply following preprogrammed rules. Nonetheless,
the obstacles many managers seem to encounter with this new
approach to strategic control probably are more emotional than
intellectual. They stem from the belief that reasoning according to
step-by-step rules and manipulating large amounts of detailed information are the best, or even the only, methods to employ in
strategic thinking.

The current received wisdom on strategic thinking is that it
is primarily an intellectual exercise in exploring what is likely to
happen. It is an exercise in information processing, in analysis, and
in forecasting future outcomes. This belief can be correct only in
regard to systems whose behavior is predictable.

Since, as we have shown, trying to predict the future is a
pointless exercise for an innovative company, strategic thinking in
such a company requires a different approach. It must be based
firmly on the qualitative nature of what is happening now and
what has happened in the past. It means focusing on anomalies in
the current situation. It means generating new perspectives on what
has been and is going on. It means framing problems and oppor-

tunities. It means noticing potential and possibility. It means noticing, as Alan Sugar did, that plastic covers for record players are being made inefficiently by one process when a more efficient process is available. It means observing the potential for developing an integrated parcel delivery system to replace a fragmented, ineffective one, as Fred Smith of Federal Express did. Note how both Alan Sugar and Fred Smith used anomalies already present to create opportunities; they did not have to envision future states. Strategic thinking is using analogies and qualitative similarities to develop creative new ideas in the here and now, not vainly trying to predict the unknowable. When we examine the analytical and analogical approaches to strategic thinking in more detail, we can see why only the analogical approach can succeed in dealing with open-ended, long-term issues.

The Analytical Approach

In the analytical approach to strategic thinking, which has been shaped by traditional scientific methodology, we focus on cause and effect. For example, we may analyze the structure of the industry in which our company operates: the barriers to entry of new firms, the availability of substitutes for our product, the power of our suppliers and customers, the intensity of the competition we face, and so on. We then identify the particular combinations of these factors that appear to have caused success for other companies in following strategies of, say, cost leadership, product differentiation, or focus on niche markets. Having identified cause and successful effect, we choose a strategy for our own business. Techniques designed to aid in the analytical approach to strategy include value chain analysis, product life cycles, product portfolio analysis, learning curves, and many more.

The contingency approach to strategic thinking also relies on perception of direct cause-and-effect relationships. Followers of this approach conclude that industries in environments with particular features such as rapid growth and high levels of uncertainty require flexible, organic organizational structures to achieve success. On the other hand, companies dealing with mature markets and low levels of uncertainty require more formal, mechanistic structures. A similar approach refers to styles of strategic management instead of structures. Its adherents state that conditions such as highly uncertain markets, overlapping portfolios of businesses, or production processes requiring investments with long-term paybacks require a "strategic management" style, which features top-down formal planning, for success. Success under other conditions, such as stable markets, portfolios of separate businesses, and short-payback investments, requires a "financial control" style, with an emphasis on tight short-term budgetary controls.[6] In both cases environmental conditions are seen as causes that require a certain structure or management style to be chosen (effect).

The analytical approach leads to general predictions and prescriptions that are to be applied in many specific instances. Managers who use these approaches recognize that their predictions and prescriptions must be only approximate because of the inability to specify models completely accurately or to take all relevant factors into account. Still, they believe that their models are general enough to be applied approximately to many different companies and still yield useful results.

When managers actually use these analytical techniques in specific situations, however, it is all too easy to make serious mistakes. In the 1970s, for example, General Foods used a technique called the Boston Grid to develop strategic options. This technique consists of rules for classifying products into categories, each of which is linked to an appropriate generic strategy. One category of products is called a "cash cow," and the appropriate strategy is one of withdrawing cash from the business; no further investment is made because "cash cows" are unexciting mature products. When General Foods applied the rules, its coffee products fell into the "cash cow" category, and investment funds were therefore withheld from the coffee products. The competitors, however, began to segment the market into specialist types of coffee. They invested in new brands for which they could charge higher prices and so earn higher margins. Almost too late, General Foods woke up to what was going on and abandoned the "cow" strategy. General strategic techniques were almost the undoing of its coffee business.

The Analogical Approach

When we think of a successful business as having chaotic dynamics, we stop looking for specific causes and effects that will lead to general prescriptions. Instead we look for the irregular but recognizable qualitative patterns of chaos—that is, analogies—as prompts to creative choices.

Everyone uses analogies based on experience in one time or place to draw conclusions about possible actions in another time or place. We do this, for instance, when we form expectations of the behavior of a group of people at some time, based on experience of another group at another time. We know the experiences will not be exactly the same, but we have reason to think that there will be some similarity. As management consultants move from one assignment to another, they accumulate models of general personality types and general group interactions. When they see a highly authoritarian manager, for example, they expect either submissive or rebellious interactions. They have no idea how these interactions will develop in specific terms, but they are not completely surprised at the outcomes.

Instead of reasoning in direct cause-and-effect terms, creative managers use strategic analysis techniques to generate analogies to their own situation. They use categories of strategic behavior, such as cost leadership or differentiation, to prompt questions and raise issues related to the specific action they are considering. They look at patterns of development as companies move from small, entrepreneurial businesses to more bureaucratic corporations, and they use these typical patterns to generate perspectives that they can use to guide the choices they must make in particular circumstances. When they do this, I suggest, they are recognizing the general, qualitative patterns that are part of chaos and using them to prompt and provoke a range of choices that they should consider. Research produced on businesses is most useful, not for analysis of direct cause-and-effect links, but for providing qualitative descriptions of patterns of behavior.

An example of how business analysts can use analogies and qualitative patterns creatively is provided, I believe, by Sioshansi's study of changes occurring in the electricity industry in North

America and Europe.[7] Sioshansi puts forward the proposition that electricity suppliers will increasingly differentiate their product. There is no definitive model that would allow someone to predict that such differentiation will occur or what form it will take. Sioshansi therefore looks for similar circumstances in other forms of business and translates the patterns observed there into ones that might apply to electricity. He cites the airline industry as one possible analogy. Like the electricity industry, this industry sells a product that cannot be stored and for which demand moves from sharp peaks to deep troughs on a daily basis. Airlines have differentiated their products by category of passenger (business and tourist), by time of use (peak and off peak), and by level of service (first class and economy). Sioshansi argues that electricity suppliers have been doing much the same thing in terms of customer category and time of use and that they could take this differentiation much further. For example, they might introduce a category of low-cost, low-service electricity with interruptible supply. This is not a prediction of what will happen but a guide that managers in the electricity industry can consider when trying to decide on creative changes for their business.

Like analysts such as Sioshansi, creative managers use analogies based on qualitative similarities to previous experience when they develop new mental models to design actions for each new strategic situation they confront. They must, however, continually reexamine, reflect upon, and reinterpret that experience to make sure that it represents a valid analogy for the new situation.

Seeing a System as a Whole

The model of strategic thinking presented by the planning and visionary approaches is essentially reductionist: it prescribes thinking processes in which the problems and opportunities to be dealt with are split into their constituent parts. In this approach, managers think about each separate part of a business, identifying key success factors, generating action options, and then selecting appropriate actions for each part. They analyze each market segment, identifying each element of its structure. They reason about the

opportunities and threats each segment presents and select a suitable focus. They then analyze each function of the business and each
aspect of its resource capability, identifying strengths and weaknesses and considering how capability needs to be matched to
market requirements. The result of this kind of thinking is embodied in hierarchies of plans for business units and for their functions,
which aggregate together into the corporate plan.

In the visionary mode, managers think in terms of an overarching vision. They then identify particular steps that can be taken
to realize that vision. They think about the consequences of those
actions before they proceed to the next ones. Thinking proceeds in
a straight line, relating cause to effect and behavior to outcome.

The study of complex, dynamic systems provides the insight
that the behavior of a system cannot be understood simply by examining the system's parts. The system in effect has a life of its own.
The system itself has a major impact on behavior and therefore on
outcomes. Thinking therefore has to proceed in terms of whole
systems, their interconnections, and the patterns of behavior they
may generate.[8] Changes accumulate slowly out of the interconnections between a system's parts. Focusing on snapshots of the parts,
looking for cause-and-effect links that are close together in time and
space, means missing the slow accumulation of change. Instead of
trying to understand the quantitative detail of the parts, therefore,
it is far more fruitful to try to understand the qualitative nature of
interconnections and patterns of behavior. It is especially helpful to
try to find the points in the system that are most sensitive and
amplifying—the points of greatest leverage. By operating at these
points rather than trying to control details everywhere, managers
can bring about the greatest changes in the system with the least
effort. These points about systems thinking were discussed in
greater detail in Chapter Two.

Thinking in system terms brings three important insights.
The first is that when things go wrong, this may be due to system
complexity; no particular individual may be to blame. The second
insight is that an individual nonetheless can make a big difference
because the structure of the system may amplify an individual contribution out of all proportion. The third insight is that operating
in complex systems that no one individual fully understands makes

both group cooperation and the sharing of different perspectives vital.

Two Kinds of Learning

Human beings can carry out at least two kinds of learning: simple, single-loop learning and complex, double-loop learning. We perform single-loop thinking and learning when we solve clear-cut problems. We develop a solution and then we test the solution. We perform an action and then learn from the outcome of the action. Feedback in single-loop learning runs from actions to outcomes and back to responding actions. When we perform this kind of learning, we use existing mental models, assumptions, and techniques without questioning or change. This is the learning mode most of us use most frequently. Managers use it when they monitor their actions against a plan, learn about the effects of their actions, and then take corrective actions. They use it when they follow a vision without questioning the assumptions on which their actions are based or the manner in which they are learning.

When we perform complex or double-loop learning, however, we question a mental model and the assumptions behind it as well as examining the problem itself. The process of posing questions becomes more important than finding answers or producing outcomes. In this kind of learning we try to look from a different perspective and frame problems and opportunities in a different way. In doing so we develop new mental models for newly perceived situations. Managers perform this kind of learning when they identify and develop an innovation. For example, Ibuka, one of the founders of Sony, questioned the assumption that radios had to weigh ten or twenty pounds and came up with the pocket-sized radio. He also questioned the assumption that mini-televisions would not sell. Kobayishi, also of Sony, questioned assumptions about organizational structures and produced a cell structure of vertically and horizontally interconnected teams. Complex learning is the form relevant to strategic situations, the form that allows us to cope with the chaos required for creativity.

An important point about complex learning is that it cannot be controlled from outside. One can instruct a group of people to

learn some simple rote task, technique, or body of data and ensure
that they do it by testing them and then rewarding or punishing
them according to the results. It is not possible to compel any group
of people to learn anything more complex than this, however. A
successful, innovative organization must have groups of people
who can perform complex learning spontaneously. Because in
open-ended situations no one can know what the group is trying
to learn, the learning process must start without a clear statement
of what is to be learned or how. Purpose and method are two of the
things the group must learn as they go along.

Studies have shown that, when managers confront open-
ended situations, they display a very widespread tendency to use
single-loop learning, which is appropriate only in closed and contained situations.[9] They seldom activate the second loop of reflecting upon the implications of action outcomes for the manner in
which those outcomes are interpreted or the frame of reference being
used. But when consequences are unknowable and cause-and-effect
links extremely unclear, it becomes vital to inquire into the manner
in which one is perceiving what is going on. Many problems that
managers have with strategic thinking may be traced to their use of
an inappropriate kind of learning.

The Impact of Group Behavior on Learning

Learning in open-ended situations has to be a group process, not
a task carried out by an individual expert or visionary. No one
individual is likely to possess wide enough perspectives to handle
such a complex situation. Such perspectives can be developed only
through group interaction.

Group interaction, not analytical thinking ability, determines whether managers attend to open-ended issues, what issues
they attend to, and what conclusions they reach. Part of an effective
double-loop learning process therefore involves continual examination of the ways in which a group is interacting. In all my strategy
consultancy assignments, the real problems have proven to have
very little to do with information or analysis or individual intellectual abilities. They have always arisen from the learning problems
caused by interaction among managers. Yet the managers involved

rarely see these matters as an essential part of the process of strategic management. Such things are parceled off as "organization behavior" or "change management," as if these were separate areas of concern.

Interactive thinking, learning, and choosing in a group is governed by feedback loops that can have either amplifying or damping properties. For example, a comment made by one member can irritate another, who responds, perhaps, by attack on some other front or by withdrawal from the discussion. Because of this, the outcome of the group interaction—the group's learning—owes much to chance. What happens during meetings therefore is often very difficult to explain. A well-timed remark, or even a purely random one, may divert the whole course of the discussion and the approach to the issue in completely different and unexpected directions. Small interventions may escalate and have a major impact.

An example of group interaction during complex learning was provided by a group of top managers in one of the United Kingdom's electricity companies that was about to be privatized. Those managers were exploring ways of improving the margins they could earn on their electricity product. Since electricity can be considered to be a commodity, they were discussing possibilities for differentiating it.

The situation they found themselves in was open-ended in just about every respect. The kind of electricity market they had to operate in had never existed before and did not exist anywhere else in the world. The chief executive started the discussion by drawing attention to a study (the one by Sioshansi mentioned earlier in this chapter) that drew parallels between differentiation of airline products and possible differentiation in electricity. Two other colleagues then joined in and started talking about the technology that would be necessary to differentiate electricity by time of use. The discussion proceeded for some time before one of the quietest members of the group suggested that the whole basis of the comparison between airlines and electricity was invalid. That interjection opened up the way for colleagues who had not expressed their views. Then one of the more vociferous group members suggested that differentiation could best be secured by adding customer features such as installation of appliances. He attached this issue to the need for coordinated marketing. The other group members saw this as his bid for increased power, and the discussion switched to organizational matters. The discussion on the very ambitious and ill-structured issue of differentiation was resumed only at a later meeting. Concrete proposals for product differentiation gradually emerged.

These managers were learning, in a group context, about a very complex strategic issue. Their somewhat random process of discussion served the valuable function of bringing different perspectives to bear on the issue. Eventually, the proposals that emerge from processes such as this might attract support. Alternatively, the whole idea might be abandoned after wide-ranging discussion. In my experience this example is typical of the early stages of handling strategic issues. Out of initial wide-ranging and random discussion emerge more precise requirements for information and proposals for action. That initial, random stage can go on for a long time. There is nothing predetermined about it; it depends upon spontaneous self-organization.

Group Composition: Personality Types

The nature of a group learning experience depends on who participates by making comments, asking questions, or donating interpretations. It depends on the content of such contributions and also on the context and sequence in which they occur. It depends on the culture that the group has developed—the basic assumptions the members of the group share on how to proceed, on how things are to be done, on what is important and what is not.[10] It depends on the combination of personalities in the group, on the emotions contributing to and provoking their interactions, on triggers to the unconscious mind. High levels of uncertainty, lack of structure, and insecurity are all known to lead to bizarre group behaviors that can prevent that group from learning.[11]

The mix of personality types in a group is important because different personalities react to the challenge of complex learning in different ways. Some people are comfortable with open-ended issues, while others look for high degrees of analytical security before they are willing to discuss an issue. Some personality types prefer to keep options open, while others always look for immediate closure. Some personality types think intuitively, and others rely heavily on formal logic. Some rely on feelings, while others always want the facts. The learning styles of individuals consequently differ markedly.

The kinds of issues a given group will deal with, what they will try to avoid, the manner in which they deal with the issues they do attend to, and how successful they are thus will depend significantly on the personality composition of the group. Small changes in personality composition, such as the removal of one person or the addition of another, can have a major impact on the outcome of the group's work together. One person behaving in a neurotic manner can completely disrupt the work of a group. These significant effects of group composition help to explain why the outcomes of complex group learning are unpredictable.

Defense Routines

The most important obstacles to complex group learning are the defense routines of the group members. These routines frequently become embedded in organizational behavior and can be extremely difficult to change. [12]

Managers who design their actions using a single-loop learning model approach a group learning experience with the assumptions that they are there to win and not lose, that they should secure unilateral control of the group situation, and that at the same time they should suppress any emotions, especially negative ones, about colleagues and their motives. This last assumption is made on the belief that people should make choices in a rational manner untainted with emotion and that expression of negative feelings will make others defensive and turn them into opponents.

When everyone in a group approaches their task with this same set of assumptions, all tend to adopt the tactics of persuasion and selling, only superficially listening to each other. They also use face-saving devices for themselves and each other and avoid publicly testing the assumptions they are making about each other's motives or statements. This behavior blocks complex learning and leads to skilled incompetence.

The most important defense routine is to make matters undiscussable and to make the fact that they are undiscussable itself undiscussable. Thus subordinates refrain from telling their superiors the truth if they think their superiors will dislike such truth—yet the subordinates do not publicly admit that they are doing this. Ask a group of managers if they tell their bosses the truth, and the usual response is raucous laughter at your naiveté; this particular defense routine is widespread indeed. At the same time, of course, superiors know that this is going on because they do it themselves. The result is an undiscussed game of pretense in which all indulge and all know they are doing it. This routine does, at least, provide work for consultants. Because superiors know that their subordinates will not tell them the truth, they hire consultants to interview and hold workshops with their subordinates. The bosses know that their subordinates are more likely to open up to outsiders.

Defense routines also include bypasses, cover-ups, and other games. For example, a manager may ask a colleague with whom he or she disagrees for comprehensive proof of a proposal outcome, when it is quite clear to all that such proof is impossible to provide. On one occasion I took part in a bypass game of this sort that went on for nearly a year. One faction thought that the company should diversify the range of its activities, while another faction, led by the chairman, thought that it should not. The chairman did not openly quash the idea, however. Instead, he called for a paper setting out general diversification principles. After discussion at the formal executive meeting, specific proposals were called for because the principles paper was held to be too general. When the specific proposals were produced, the chairman called for a discussion of the general principles—and so it went on. Needless to say, no diversification occurred. Everyone involved knew it was a game, but although we admitted this to each other in groups of two or three, no one ever mentioned it at the full meetings.

As soon as we recognize that the dynamic of a successful company is chaotic and the long-term future is unknowable, it becomes clear that long-term plans, mission statements, and visions are also bypass games. These abstract statements without operational content, are produced simply to convey an impression of rational decision making and to keep people quiet or secure.

Perhaps the most popular cover-up, usually done unconsciously, is to say one thing while doing another. Thus, managers
may say they are looking for team decision making, that they are
open to different views, and then become visibly annoyed when any
such views are put forward. Their behavior makes it clear that team
decision making is not actually going to occur despite any statements they make.

These kinds of defensive behavior become so entrenched in
organizations that they come to be viewed as an inevitable part of
human nature. Managers make self-fulfilling prophecies about
what will happen at meetings concerned with open-ended issues:
because they expect game playing, they themselves indulge in it,
thus confirming their belief in human nature. Defense routines can
become so disruptive that managers may try to avoid discussing
contentious, open-ended issues altogether in order to avoid them.
Even if this extreme is not reached, the dysfunctional behavior
blocks any real discussion or examination of either new proposals
or old frameworks. Under these circumstances, managers struggling
to deal with strategic issues end up preparing long lists of strengths
and weaknesses, meaningless mission statements, or long-term
plans that are simply filed.

Managers collude in this behaviour and refrain from discussing it. They then distance themselves from what is going on and
blame others or the system when things go wrong. They look for
solutions in general models, techniques, visions, and plans, while
the real causes of poor strategic management—poor choices of
learning process and dysfunctional political interaction and group
dynamics—remain stubbornly undiscussable.

When managers do try seriously to grapple with what is
going on, their most common response is to swing to the complete
opposite of the single-loop learning model just described. They try
to work on the assumption that everyone should be involved in
everything, that all should win, that feelings and emotions should
be freely expressed. Behaving on these assumptions immobilizes
decision making and learning just as effectively as the opposite
forms of behavior. The reasons for this are quite simple. Involving
everyone in everything simply slows decision making down and
leads to confusion. In complex situations, it is impossible for every-

one to win—some must lose. Freely expressing emotions and assertions about other people will simply lead to unnecessary conflict.

Group Dynamics

Group dynamics are the behavior and interaction of a group as a
whole. One well-known study explains the behavior of a group in
terms of two levels.[13] At one level, the conscious apparent level, the
group is focusing on the work in hand, the tasks it has come together to perform. But at the unconscious level, the behavior of
individuals in the group is affected by a basic assumption, an atmosphere that affects how they work together. For example, they
may be unconsciously affected by the fight-flight assumption. Here
the underlying dynamic is one of either intense conflict or the complete avoidance of conflict. Alternatively, the assumption may be
one of dependence, where the group is looking for leadership. Or
it may be one of pairing, in which most of the group is observing
an interchange between two of their number, hoping that this will
yield the answer they are looking for.

Different basic assumptions are appropriate to different
tasks. When the group is concerned with simple, unambiguous
matters, a basic assumption of dependence and the compliance that
accompanies this will make it more effective. When the group is
concerned with open-ended issues, however, a basic assumption
that results in some conflict is more likely to be helpful. When
structures are removed and the group faces considerable uncertainty, the basic assumptions can come to dominate behavior in the
group so completely that it is incapable of any work at all. Under
these circumstances, too, a group can switch suddenly from one
basic assumption to another.

Situations involving open-ended change are the ones most
likely to provoke group dynamics that obstruct dealing with the
issues. Groups cannot deal with open-ended issues while they are
dominated by the fight-flight assumption, for example. Groups
showing a high level of dependence may not develop wide enough
perspectives to handle such issues effectively.

It is not unusual for managers to abandon meetings trying
to deal with open-ended issues because such meetings simply do not

function. One of my clients, in the electronics industry, called an informal meeting of top executives to discuss reorganization proposals. The group accomplished nothing in two days of meetings because they did little but fight over the proposals. That chief executive thereafter avoided such informal meetings. On another occasion, the first two strategy workshops I facilitated with a top management team consisted mostly of the others listening to a discussion between the chief executive and myself. It was only when we brought in other people that the dynamics changed. On another occasion in the same industry, faced with massive changes, the top team avoided any serious issues throughout three meetings. The underlying conflict between them made it too dangerous to talk about any of the issues in a serious way.

The key to effective strategic management is creating group dynamics that encourage participation in the second learning loop. This involves making explicit and exploring not only the issues themselves but also the learning behaviors, defense routines, and personal interactions engaged in by group members and trying to identify the mental models that have led to the way problems and opportunities are being framed. The second loop means developing a different learning model and changing mind-sets. The behavior here is one of openness, real listening, and a readiness to change one's mind. Individuals engaging in successful double-loop learning strongly advocate their positions but at the same time invite others to test those positions. They describe the motives that they attribute to others and offer evidence for those attributions. The result is not a free-for-all display of feelings and emotions but a disciplined attempt to reveal and test the undiscussable matters that could be blocking the learning process.

Changing group dynamics and developing more useful learning habits is a difficult, time-consuming, and sometimes personally threatening process. There are no general prescriptions, just as there are no general prescriptions a neurotic individual can follow to cure his or her own neurosis. Just as the individual has to work with a therapist in a manner dictated by the specific circumstances, so a group of managers intent on improving their group learning skills will need to work with a consultant in a manner dictated by their specific circumstances.

People do not provoke new insights when their discussions are characterized by orderly equilibrium, conformity, and dependence. Neither do they do so when their discussions enter the explosively unstable equilibrium of all-out conflict or complete avoidance of the issues. Complex group learning occurs only when the feedback loops governing the learning keep the group far from equilibrium. People spark new ideas off each other when they argue and disagree—when they are conflicting, confused, and searching for a new meaning—yet remain willing to discuss and listen to each other. These are the only group dynamics suitable for handling open-ended issues.

New Emphases in Strategic Thinking

Understanding a business in terms of dynamic feedback systems provides a new perspective on the nature of strategic thinking and learning. This perspective focuses attention on the group learning process, the assumptions driving that process, and the deeply embedded organizational obstacles to that process rather than on analytical techniques. It results in the following major shifts in emphasis:

- Away from a concern with the individual expert or visionary and toward a concern with the effects of the personalities, group dynamics, and learning behaviors of managers in groups
- Away from the stability of continuing consensus based on "rational" reasoning and toward the creative instability of contention and dialogue, with periodic consensus concerning particular issues
- Away from condemning the messiness of real-life business decision making as dysfunctional politics and then ignoring it, toward examining, understanding, and dealing with organizational defense mechanisms and game playing
- Away from the perception of group learning as a simple process relating to outcomes and toward an understanding of group learning as a complex process of continually questioning how people are learning

- Away from the closure of problem solving, and toward the opening up of contentious and ambiguous issues
- Away from trying to apply general prescriptive models to many specific situations and toward developing new mental models to design actions for each new strategic situation

In the last chapter, we looked at broad phases in the way managers handle agendas of strategic agendas. In this chapter, we considered the nature of the thinking processes they bring to bear on those issues. In the next chapter, we turn to the role of shared intention in the handling of strategic issues.

6

Strategic Agendas: Deciphering the Patterns in Goals and Actions

Most practical people believe that order and creativity appear in human societies as the result of deliberate design and will. Organizations, most believe, develop successfully because some individual or group of individuals consciously intends a particular state to occur and persuades others to assist in realizing that state. Thus, when Hamel and Prahalad (see Chapter Two) research the model of strategic management that leads Japanese managers to success, they identify strategic intent as the key to that success. When Senge (see Chapter Two) researches a number of successful American companies, he equates success with the ability of an organization to learn and claims that a key element in that ability is the vision of the organization's managers. Tom Peters[1] also consistently links the vision of charismatic leaders to subsequent outstanding business performance. Study after study confirms the importance for success of forming a vision well in advance of acting; that is, of establishing organizational intention, or deliberate predetermined agreement by a company's top managers in regard to a whole set of key issues.

Does this agreement among researchers arise because vision and intention really are important for success, or is it merely a reflection of the frame of reference within which these researchers approach their task? Do managers so readily accept the recommendation to form a vision because it is a practical proposition, or do they do so because it allows them to erect a comfortable defense against examining more threatening requirements of successful management?

The old but still dominant view about the importance of intention in human systems has not been without its critics. The Nobel prize-winning economist Friederich von Hayek[2] argued many years ago that human institutions evolve as a result of human action, not human intention. Markets develop, he explained, because entrepreneurs create possibilities that their customers did not know existed before. No one can predict the emergence of new knowledge—original ideas and innovations—or the reactions of people to it. Markets are systems for discovering emergent patterns, not realizing human intentions.

Karl Weick[3] presented similar arguments over twenty years ago. He described human organizations as systems so complex that no actor within them can fully understand how they work. However, actors within such systems make contributions, relying on others to do the same, and together they create emergent patterns that would have been beyond the capability of any one of them either to intend or to realize. Any overall shared intention can be identified only after the event, through the benefit of hindsight.

More recently, some writers have claimed that strategy in fact emerges from tactics rather than vice versa.[4] Others see strategy formation as a revolution in what the company does rather than a series of incremental actions[5] or as the ideas and actions of individual organizational actors that converge on a common theme.[6] All these interpretations stress patterns in action that emerge or evolve over the long term from convergent behavior and collective action in the absence of prior central intention, grand designs, or continuing central control.[7]

Pascale (see Chapter Two) provides some empirical evidence for this kind of explanation in his account of the successful transformation of Ford Motor Company in the 1980s from a huge loss maker to a profitable and widely acclaimed company. This transformation is the story of a number of independent individual intentions and actions—initiatives on quality, design, employee participation, executive development, studies on Japanese competitors, management workshops, and many more—that somehow came together in a mutually reinforcing way. All of this happened in conditions of conflict and tension, without a central plan or vision.

Pascale describes what happened as the coincident unfolding of events, with the coincidence being impossible to envision without the benefit of hindsight.

These explanations and pieces of evidence are usually dismissed, however, as armchair philosophizing; they have made hardly any impact upon the thinking of practical business people. Practical people, it seems, still adhere to the view that nature follows fixed laws with a clockwork precision that makes it foolish to talk about creative natural systems, whereas human systems move in creative ways determined by the purpose and intention of their principal members.

The great importance of the discoveries about nonlinear feedback systems—that is, about chaos (outlined in Chapter Three) and self-organization (outlined in Chapter Four)—is that they make this whole worldview completely untenable. We now know that most of nature's systems are nonlinear feedback ones that function in many respects in a chaotic, and therefore unpredictable, continuously creative manner that makes simple ideas of controlling them impractical. Furthermore, as I have argued in this book, human organizations also are quite clearly nonlinear feedback systems that must operate in chaos if they are to be continually creative. This means that the long-term future of such organizations is completely unknowable because the links between specific actions and specific outcomes become lost in the detail of what happens. We can claim to have achieved something intentionally only when we can show that there was a connection between the specific action we took and the specific state we achieved; in other words, that what we achieved was not materially affected by chance. Since it is impossible to satisfy this condition when we operate in a chaotic system, it follows that successful human organizations cannot be the realization of some shared intention formed well ahead of action. Instead, success has to be the discovery of patterns that emerge through actions we take in response to the changing agendas of issues we identify. The only escape from this conclusion is to reject the idea that successful organizations are chaotic self-organizing systems, and the arguments presented in Chapters Three and Four make this difficult to do.

This question of intentional realization versus the discovery of emergent pattern is so important because the answer we give to that question has a major impact on the actions we take. If we believe that nature's systems function like clockwork and human systems move to the dictates of designing minds, we quite naturally believe that nature can be controlled once the laws governing it have been discovered and human systems can be redesigned from scratch once a new intention has been formed. The prescription for action is clear: form a vision of the future state we desire to achieve, persuade others to believe in it as well, and then together, if we get our facts right, we will be able to realize it. In this view, top management action will take the form of trying to find out in advance what is likely to happen. Managers will prepare forecasts, and they will go off for weekends to formulate visions and missions. They will mount comprehensive culture change programs of persuasion and propaganda to get people throughout the organization to commit to a new vision. But if the belief upon which these actions are based is unfounded, they will have wasted their time and probably missed doing what was really necessary for success.

If, on the other hand, we believe that systems in both nature and human society are creative when they operate in chaos, we will see that it is impossible to be "in control" of the future of such systems or to redesign them from scratch. We will understand that people interacting in an organization may produce a pattern in their actions through self-organization, provided that the context in which they work enables them to discover and learn. Top management action arising from this view will take the form of looking for and removing obstacles to effective political interaction and learning in the present. The focus for action will shift from speculation about the future to dealing with current issues that have long-term consequences, from persuasion and propaganda to learning and discovery. The focus will be on detecting anomalies in what is going on now, using intuition and analogy to develop responses, and examining and trying to improve the group dynamics upon which such processes in organizations depend.

The question of the role of intention and vision in strategic management is therefore one of great practical importance. This chapter will examine it in some detail.

Strategy as "Vision"

Terms used, often interchangeably, to denote a range of concepts vital to discussions on the role of intention in strategic management include *vision, values, dream, mission, strategic intent, business philosophy, culture, company recipe, mental model,* and *frame of reference.* All of these terms basically describe three different concepts. Sometimes one term covers all three concepts; in other cases, authors use different terms for each. Frequently the terms are used so loosely that it is not clear what concept they refer to. The three concepts are as follows:

- The future state or destination of the business—a pattern of what is to be
- The drivers or motivators of business behavior—a pattern of becoming
- The business philosophy, culture, or shared beliefs about what the business is there for, what it is, why it is as it is, what makes it successful, and how people in it should behave—a pattern of being

Let us further consider each of these concepts and what recent discoveries about dynamic systems have to say about each concept's usefulness in strategic management. We will see that it is impossible to form a useful picture of a future state for a creative business system; that it is harmful to focus attention on single motivators to drive behavior when times are turbulent; and that it is impossible to install a business philosophy from scratch and highly dangerous to persuade all in a business to agree on a single philosophy. Instead, people in creative organizations are driven by many challenges arising in the present; they question the existing philosophy and even destroy aspects of it to make way for the new.

Vision as a Picture of the Future

The first sense in which *vision* and related terms are used has to do with what the business is to be at some point in the long-term future. It is a reasonably fixed, unique destination—what those in charge of the business want to achieve. Those who prescribe formation of such a vision as the first step in effective strategic management[8] speak of it as a realistic future state that represents a desirable improvement over the present—a state that has never existed before. It is said to provide an overarching goal for the business, covering all the most important issues that will confront the organization and governing the way these issues are to be dealt with. It must be shared by all managers over time; only its peripheral aspects are to be questioned or challenged. It must be specific enough to be acted upon, yet general enough to allow bold initiative. It is a unanimous, unique answer to the question, "What do we intend to be in the future?"

From the preceding description it can be seen that six important properties must be present if a vision is to function as the intention that drives a whole organization to an identified destination in the future. Let us consider each of these properties and what it means in a creative feedback system.

A Vision Must Be Specific and Unique

First, the vision must be a desired or imagined future state that, if it is realized, stands a good chance of improving on what currently exists. Business organizations succeed when they are different from their rivals, so the desired state must be unique in some sense if it is to be the cause of success. It must also be reasonably specific if it is to indicate what actions are to be undertaken to achieve it.

In practice, managers often have considerable difficulty in formulating visions that are unique and specific enough. Indeed, managers frequently choose almost painfully obvious "visions." For example, in the case described in Chapter Two, the managers chose a vision of their company as the "Innovators." But because the market game nowadays is fast moving, highly competitive, and uncertain, it surely requires innovative behavior from any successful player. Therefore it is difficult to see how the "Innovators" vision will differentiate this company from any of its successful rivals. Other common company visions focus on beating the competition, caring for customers, or delivering quality goods and high levels of service. Again, these are concerns every company must attend to if it wishes to survive. They are continuing rules of the game, not long-term objectives toward which a company should be moving. If a business is not doing these things already, it probably will not have a long term. Statements about these matters may function as important motivators, a matter we turn to in the next section, but they do not provide specific, unique desired states for the future.

Why do managers so frequently produce bland statements that are the same as those of their competitors when they are asked to formulate a vision? Perhaps it is because they realize that there is a thin line dividing a more specific and unique vision from a fantasy. We are free to desire and imagine whatever we wish, whether we are part of a creative system or not. If, however, those desires and images are to be more than fantasies, they must possess another important property.

A Vision Must Be Anchored to Reality

A vision must be anchored to reality in some way if it is to be more than a fantasy. In other words, the desired and imagined state must be achievable in the future time period during which it is to be realized. This in turn means that managers must be able to predict enough about a specific future time period to make it possible to reach the conclusion that a particular vision is achievable.

This requirement cannot be satisfied for a nonlinear feedback system operating in chaos because the very structure of such a system makes it impossible to predict any long-term future state: the future for such a system is unknowable, and we therefore can say nothing useful about any specific long-term future point for that system. Because successful organizations are nonlinear feedback systems operating in chaos, they cannot be driven according to a vision that is anchored to a future reality. All we can know is that the future will display familiar, recognizable patterns of a qualitative kind that will emerge from our actions and that we will be able to make sense of them as the basis for further action. We cannot know which patterns will emerge, but we can be confident that we will be able to deal with them when we encounter them because of the way we think, a matter already discussed in Chapter Five.

A Vision Must Be Linked to Action

Third, if organizational intention is to be useful, it must be possible to link a realistic desired future state back to the actions required to produce it. Put another way, if we are to achieve a vision intentionally, we will have to be able to know the specific long-term consequences of our actions before we take them. If we have to act without knowing the long-term consequences of our actions, then what happens will emerge partly by chance rather than materialize from intention. In a chaotic system such as a creative organization, however, the links between cause and effect are lost in the detail of what happens. We therefore cannot identify the actions required to realize any envisioned outcome.

Take the weather system as an example. This system, like a successful business, operates in conditions of bounded instability, so we cannot intervene to change the weather to a specific state we desire. For example, we cannot intervene to produce an extra three inches of rainfall next month because we cannot know what the rainfall would have been without our intervention. But we can know that next month is usually, say, one of low rainfall. We can foresee a qualitative pattern of this kind. Can we then intervene to make next month a high-rainfall one instead? The answer is still no, because the very nature of the system means that any intervention we make could have escalating and unpredictable consequences. Instead of a high-rainfall month our intervention might provoke a flood or a drought. Because of escalation, that is, weak links between cause and effect, we cannot know the result of our intervention in either quantitative or qualitative terms until we have intervened. It is possible to seed clouds and produce some local rain, but those doing this have no idea of the more distant weather effects their intervention might touch off. No matter how much we improve technology or our understanding of the weather system, we will not be able to make long-term forecasts because the system will always escalate changes so tiny that we could never measure them; the tiny change we inevitably miss will alter the whole future course of the system, thus nullifying our attempts to control it. We will be able to recognize general patterns, but we cannot say which patterns they will be until the consequences of our intervention have worked themselves out.

Without the ability to link present and future through dependable cause and effect, a vision is useless as a guide to strategy. In view of this, it is not surprising to find that the advice on how to form a vision is, to say the least, vague. Vision, supposed to be the prime concern of the leaders of an organization, is to be formed by listening to others, observing what is going on, and trying to find clues that suggest how the world will change. Creation of a vision is said to involve some rational analysis, but it is also intuitive, a creative leap of the imagination. In other words, no one really knows how we are supposed to form a vision.

We may, of course, imagine or desire a future state without knowing anything at all about the future in which it is to be realized or anything about how it is to be realized, and yet not be guilty of mere fantasizing, provided that the image or desire is realistic in current circumstances. This, however, is exactly what an aspiration, ambition, or challenge is. The fulfillment of an aspiration occurs at a time in the future, but the aspiration itself relies on the present for that connection with reality that distinguishes it from a fantasy. We will discuss aspirations and ambitions in the next section; they do not qualify as pictures of a future state because they are not anchored to the reality of a future state. The important distinction is that to drive a business to a future state we have to know something about that future state, but to drive a business with ambitions and aspirations from the present we do not need to know anything at all about the future, only about the present and the past. To drive a business to an identified point located in the future we have to be able to link actions to the outcomes that will produce that point. However, to drive a business from the present by posing challenges and aspirations does not require that we link actions to outcomes; we can accept instead that outcomes will emerge from what we do in ways we are not yet clear about. What we need to do in the two cases, driving to a future state and driving by ambition from a current situation, is therefore different.

A Vision Must Be Overarching and Comprehensive

The fourth property required of a vision is that it must be overarching and comprehensive: it must cover and provide some criteria for dealing with all the most important issues that the organization will face. If this is not so, the eventual shape of the organization will emerge from the way issues chance to be handled when they occur rather than according to the organization's prior intention.

When specific strategic issues arise in practice, however, managers rarely refer back to some prior vision or plan to provide criteria for dealing with those issues. If they do, they often find that the issue that concerns them is not covered. Despite what is supposed to be a guiding framework, managers continue to handle specific strategic issues on a case-by-case basis, just as they would have to do if no long-term intention existed. In short, managers say that they have to establish shared organizationwide intentions and set out sequences of planned actions far in advance of those actions, but in fact they mostly discover both intentions and actions as they go along.

A Vision Must Be Shared by All

Fifth, the vision must be shared by all the key players in the organization if we are to talk about the intention of the organization. Otherwise, what happens will emerge from the clash between intentions expressed by different subunits. In theory, a vision comes to be shared because leaders preach their vision and convert others to it, gaining enthusiastic commitment through a mixture of charisma and discussion.

In practice, however, how do we distinguish between a healthy sharing of some sensible intention and dangerous "groupthink" in which all members of an organization cling unquestioningly to a single idea? It is obvious that clinging blindly to a vision that turns out to be wrong is dangerous. It is just as important to note, however, that such clinging is dangerous even when the vision turns out to be right. Holding unquestioningly to a successful vision promotes exactly the kind of excessive concentration on what originally led to success that Miller and Pascale conclude leads ultimately to failure. This point was discussed in Chapter Two.

When the future is open ended and unknowable, it is completely inappropriate and highly dangerous for individuals in a group to share unquestioningly the same picture of a future state. Since none of them can know the outcome—they have to discover that outcome and learn as they act—it is vital that people continually question what they are doing and why they are doing it. It will not be enough to question some commonly held view simply at the margin. Complex learning requires continual questioning of the very fundamentals of what managers are trying to do together.

A Vision Must Be Stable over Time

Finally, the shared picture of a unique future state must remain stable over time if it is to constitute organizational intention. If managers keep changing their vision, we have to conclude that they are not driving their business intentionally according to the vision but are discovering their intention as they go along.

In practice, however, when managers do establish specific long-term intentions they usually qualify them with statements such as, "These must not be written on tablets of stone." In other words, long-term intentions are to be loose; people expect that they will be changed long before the time they are meant to apply to. When managers do this, they are really discovering their intentions as they move through time rather than setting them well in advance as stable guides for action.

The dynamics of successful organizations lead us to expect that leaders will not be able to drive their businesses according to visions that meet these six criteria, yet research keeps producing the conclusion that successful businesses are driven by vision. How can this be? If we consider some examples of such research, we will see how the visions identified there fail to match the six criteria we have discussed.

Two Examples: Federal Express and Amstrad

Federal Express in the United States and Amstrad in the United Kingdom are two companies often cited as having succeeded because of the "vision" of their founders. But was this really the case?

Fred Smith, the founder of Federal Express, is said to have envisioned a future in which letters and small parcels would be delivered overnight across the United States by a private enterprise. Smith's imagined parcel delivery system consisted of air transport from dispersed collection depots to a central sorting hub, from which items would be rerouted to delivery depots, the spokes of the wheel. The realization of this "hub and spoke" vision was Federal Express, and it created a whole new market.

But was Federal Express really the result of a specifically formulated vision of a future state that was then realized? The answer is no, on two counts.

First, it is a myth that the delivery system concept sprang full-blown from the head of its founder at a single point in time. Smith expressed some of the original ideas that were to be realized as Federal Express when he wrote a college paper in 1964, but it took years to develop the whole concept. Smith's first business venture after college was selling and repairing aircraft, which certainly had little to do with overnight parcel deliveries. He continued to think about that concept, however, and in 1971 he began to develop it. He bought two jets and set up Federal Express to deliver checks for the Federal Reserve system, but the Fed backed out of the contract. Undaunted, Smith commissioned market research on parcel movements and purchased twenty-three additional aircraft. During 1971 and 1972 he lobbied the air transport regulation authorities to allow his aircraft to be used for parcel deliveries. He and his team also expended much effort in raising money for the company. Smith decided on the "hub and spoke" design of his delivery system in 1972 and made the first deliveries in a test network covering eleven cities in 1973. The operation did not make a profit, however, until 1976.[9]

Second, Fred Smith did not really foresee anything about a future state. What he observed was a current situation. He observed an existing industry for delivering letters and parcels that was fragmented, ineffective, expensive, and overregulated. He gathered information on current delivery volumes and the way deliveries were currently made. Over time he developed creative ideas about ways to improve delivery activities. He displayed great determination and took major risks in demonstrating that his ideas could work. But he did not foresee anything about the future state in which those ideas would work. In advance, he had no idea whether they would work or not. He had to find out by trying them. Nothing he did required a picture of a future state.

Smith clearly imagined something that might exist in the future and desired that this should come about. This was more than a fantasy, even back in 1964, because it was anchored to the reality of that time, specifically the anomalies in the parcel delivery systems that existed then. The picture Smith used was not of a future state but of existing anomalies. It is more accurate to say that he was driven by aspirations and challenges arising in the present rather than by something beckoning him from the future. This distinction is of great importance because if we conclude that Smith was beckoned from the future, we will advise would-be billionaires to think about the future, and in doing so they will probably miss the present anomalies that are the source of tomorrow's fortunes.

What actually happened in the development of Federal Express was not as simple as forming a vision of the future and then realizing it. Smith had an initial idea about parcel deliveries, but no one at that time knew what shape that idea would take or whether any given shape would work. Instead of a picture of a future state, Smith had only a provoking idea and a challenge. In developing this overall concept Smith and his colleagues dealt with a changing agenda of issues and challenges over time, provoked by observing current problems, and formed ideas about ways to deal with them. The issues related to the design of a more effective delivery system, the challenge of air transport regulations, and the sources of finance. As they handled these issues, often in a piecemeal fashion without an overarching picture of a future state to guide them, Smith and the others learned whether their ideas would work or not—and from that learning emerged the concept that was to be Federal Express. They were discovering both the pattern that was to be and the way to secure it; both were emerging, not preplanned or "envisioned."

To be sure, links between Smith's intention and what subsequently happened appear at first to be clear. These links, however, turn out to be so clear only with the benefit of hindsight. Such hindsight makes what happened seem more organizationally intended than it actually was. Many people have a strong tendency to use hindsight in this way because they start with a frame of reference that leads them to expect to find causal connections, whether or not such connections actually exist. The usual way of recounting the Federal Express story, therefore, could well be subject to interpretive bias.

The possibility of interpretive bias is shown by the way writers ignore "visions" that failed when they prescribe the forming of visions as the route to success. For example, Fred Smith had a second vision that met with a fate very different from that of his original Federal Express. He pictured a future in which Federal Express leased out "Zapmail" fax machines to customers linked into an expensive and complex satellite telecommunications system. Many millions of dollars later, the venture failed because cheap fax machines linked into existing telecommunications networks swept the market. This time it was rivals in another industry that created a new market.

This episode is not usually quoted as a "vision" on the part of Federal Express. It turned out to be beneficial that Federal Express managers shared Smith's first "vision" and pursued it with unquestioning determination, if that is what they did. In the case of the second "vision," however, the same behavior led to disaster. If no one is allowed to question a vision, signs of impending failure may pass unnoticed until it is too late.

Another noted visionary, this time in the United Kingdom, is Alan Sugar, who built up a major electronics business, Amstrad, within a few years. His biography does not provide any evidence of his having had some overarching vision of a future successful electronics company. Instead, the biography describes a man with an ever-changing agenda of issues that he pursued. An early issue was providing cheap plastic covers for record turntables. It was followed by integrated tower system hi-fi sets, car entertainment systems, personal computers, and satellite dishes. Accompanying all these successes, according to Sugar's biographer, were many ideas pursued for a time and then dropped because they were not successful. The biography makes it clear that the shape of the Amstrad business was not foreseen. Rather, it evolved as its founder and his colleagues pursued the discovery of opportunities and mistakes with determination and creativity. They were learning through what they did and so discovering their future state.[10]

As these examples suggest, there is little evidence that successful entrepreneurs somehow foresee future states and then proceed to realize them. What we find instead is highly energetic and hardworking people with a full agenda of issues that they are pursuing at any one time. This agenda continually changes, with some issues dropping off after little exploration, others being discontinued after either major or minor failures, and yet others being developed to the point where successful new strategies emerge. Rather than foreseeing and then realizing a future, these entrepreneurs take big risks with little idea of the outcome. Sometimes they succeed and create new markets and technologies; sometimes they fail and have to try again. Successful entrepreneurs and managers have creative, challenging ideas that arise from what they experience and observe. They explore these ideas in a determined but open-minded and continually questioning fashion. Although they cannot know the outcome, they take a chance, they accept risk, they are prepared to back their judgments.

If this is really how successful companies operate, why do researchers keep concluding that shared visions are essential to success? First, they may be using the word *vision* to mean something other than a picture of a future state; we will consider other possible meanings in later sections. Second, the evidence that visions of future states have anything to do with business success is anecdotal and conditioned by interpretive bias. This evidence consists mostly of case studies and examples (such as Federal Express and Amstrad) in which particular business successes are described in terms of some originating vision. The authors who use these examples look back in time for a vision that might be said to have started the whole venture off, and then they describe the ensuing sequence of events in terms of realization of that vision. In doing so they use hindsight to interpret selectively what actually happened and so, not surprisingly, confirm what they believed in the first place: that visions are important.

Dynamic systems theory, on the contrary, leads us to expect that managers will encounter problems when they try to form pictures of a future state and then manage according to those visions. Practice confirms this expectation.

The Dangers of Visions in Practice

To begin with, when managers are told to form a picture of a future state, most of them simply do not know what to do. The advice to form a vision is not concrete enough to be useful, nor does it produce something possible to achieve because the future is unknowable. The result of the advice, therefore, usually is simply bewilderment and frustration.

For example, take a group of divisional managers I worked with recently. The division consisted of a number of information technology companies that had been acquired a short time before. Some of these companies distributed directly to end users, while others sold products to equipment manufacturers, including their sister subsidiaries. The direct distribution companies therefore competed with the customers of the companies who distributed products indirectly. Not surprisingly, use of these two routes to market led to continual conflict between the subsidiaries. Those distributing through the indirect route complained that those distributing directly were competing unfairly because of the transfer pricing rules imposed by the division. These rules were antagonizing the customers of the subsidiaries who distributed indirectly, and those division members were therefore losing business. Clearly, the divisional management therefore either had to devise an organizational structure and transfer pricing policies that allowed both kinds of companies to operate effectively or had to abandon one of the routes to market.

To deal with the problem, the divisional managers were advised to formulate a vision or dream of what they wanted to be in the future. The mission statement they all agreed upon was to become one of the major players in the market, using both routes to market if that turned out to be the right thing to do. Given the uncertain market conditions they faced, however, none of the divisional managers felt able to formulate anything more specific than this, which was really a way of saying, "Wait and see how it turns out." Nothing in their statement indicated which structural form or what transfer pricing policy was appropriate. Thus, instructing these managers to formulate a vision had no practical usefulness and merely distracted their attention from the real issues, which had to do with the conflicting ambitions of the team members and judgments about the reactions of the equipment customers and competitors to different arrangements.

Furthermore, this advice to form a vision had a debilitating effect on some of the managers involved. The managing director of the division decided to use a workshop approach, during which middle managers could offer their views on what form the reorganization should take. The first meeting of this workshop did not reach agreement, partly because of the different assumptions that members were making about the future direction of the business. In particular, one group assumed that the firm's major future impetus would be through sales of its products directly to end users, while another assumed that the main thrust would be through indirect sales to equipment manufacturers. Both groups looked to top management to make a decision about future direction, but the top management team stated that they did not know where the future direction lay—everything was too uncertain. At the next workshop, some of the middle managers said that they found this indecision completely unacceptable; they could not see how any further work on reorganization could continue without first defining future direction. In fact, the group as a whole was able to put forward sensible proposals about reorganization to deal with the business's current problems. But some members lost their motivation, and their contribution declined, because of their belief in the need for a decision about future direction.

The second defect of the vision prescription is that if one insists that managers share an unquestioned view of their future, they must all either persist with what they already know how to do or pursue what could be a disastrous new idea in a lemminglike dash to destruction. While they are following a single vision, they will inevitably fail to notice important changes in the business.

Third, the emphasis on visions places a tremendous and unrealistic burden on leaders as well as followers. It perpetuates the myth that organizations have to rely on one or two unusually gifted individuals to decide what to do, while the rest enthusiastically follow. Reliance on visions perpetuates cultures of dependence and conformity that obstruct the questioning and complex learning necessary for innovative action.

Fourth and finally, the vision advice distracts attention from what people are really doing when they successfully handle unknowable futures—that is, learning and interacting in groups. If one talks to managers about strategy as patterns in action determined by visionary or planning activity, they immediately recognize what one is talking about. If one talks about strategy as patterns in action emerging from learning and political activity, however, one is frequently greeted with blank stares. Yet it is the latter that are actually involved in strategic management. Most managers do not consciously recognize this fact because, I suggest, their thinking is too much conditioned by models of organizational intention and stability.

Vision as Motivator

The second sense in which *vision* and related terms are used is related to motivation. This is purpose in the sense of a reason for doing what one is doing, rather than purpose in terms of what one will achieve. It is a pattern of becoming rather than a pattern in what will be. Why managers do what they do can be described in terms such as *inspirations, aspirations, ambitions, hopes, obsessions, inner standards of excellence, ideas, concepts,* and *challenges.* These words convey a sense of destiny rather than the sense of destination implied by the "future state" use of *vision.* They describe a belief in the ability to create a future without necessarily knowing what that future will look like. *Vision* in this sense is an answer to the questions, "Why am I doing what I do? Why do I want to become something different? Why and how do I want to become better?" It refers to a pattern embodied in the climate, style, or spirit of the organization. Proponents of the intentional mode of strategy formation expect these motivational aspirations or inspirations, like visions of a future state, to be intentionally set up and spread by top management.

Many examples are given of these drivers of behavior in a business. Apple is said to be driven by a desire to provide computing

for the masses. Ford was driven by the challenge of bringing transport to the masses and Coca-Cola by the aspiration to "put a Coke
in arm's reach of everyone." Polaroid's challenge was to develop
instant photography. Other examples of challenges or ambitions
relate to rivals—for example, Xerox's desire to "beat Canon" and
Komatsu's obsession to "encircle Caterpillar." Other examples of
driving forces include Honda's aspiration to become the second
Ford and to be an automotive pioneer, and NEC's ambition to
acquire technologies to be the best. Global success or unquestioned
superiority may drive other companies.

These challenges really are just specific ways of stating a
strong desire to win the competitive business game. They are usually simple, though important, restatements of the rules of the game
or distillations of the operating recipes of successful entrepreneurs.
These restatements may be important if they relate to rules of the
competition game, which have slipped from people's attention.
Restating the need for quality, or customer care, could then provide
a motivating focus for people. Komatsu's "Encircling Caterpillar,"
for example, obviously is just a statement about outcompeting a
business rival, but it no doubt had a galvanizing effect on employees. Similarly, Chapter Two referred to a business that tried to
differentiate itself from its competitors by formulating a vision of
its collective self as "The Innovators." This "vision" simply re-
stated a characteristic that all successful companies must have, but
it is possible that this image might enthuse people.

Supporters of the organizationally intended approach to
strategy formation claim that people in successful companies
strongly share the same, overarching aspiration, or view of the reason why they act as they do, in a stable manner over time. They do
not question the basic nature of this aspiration. It is part of what
provides the focus for their individual efforts and provides purpose
for the organization as a whole.

When we see a business organization as a dynamic feedback
system needing to operate in bounded instability to be continually
innovative, however, another perspective becomes evident. In order
to learn continually in turbulent environments, managers have to
keep generating and exploring many different challenges. In such
environments, where the consequences of change are unknowable

and many of the changes themselves are small and difficult to detect, challenges (both problems and opportunities) are almost sure to be ill structured and difficult to frame. Conflict about how to interpret the challenges, and about which ambitions and aspirations are appropriate to follow when responding to them, is both inevitable and desirable. In such circumstances it is detrimental for leaders to fix on some single aspiration, or some small set of them, for lengthy periods. Sharing the same aspiration blocks the complex learning required in these situations and thus, like sharing the same vision of a future state, is dangerous.

The challenges generated by business systems in open-ended situations emerge from the political interactions between managers and from what and how they are learning together. In this view the role of top management is not to invent and preach simple, clear aspirations but rather to create a context favorable to complex learning, from which challenges may emerge. Consensus about meeting a certain challenge, such as beating a certain competitor, may be achieved for a time, but this motivation will change when other challenges arise. To keep an organization on its toes, top managers should present ambiguous challenges and ambitions that are difficult to achieve so as to provoke people into thinking and arguing.

Vision as Business Philosophy or Culture

The philosophy of a business is a set of beliefs explaining why the business is what it is. It describes the purpose of the business in the sense of its reason for being, its mission. The concept includes the moral standards of the business, that is, the norms relating to the manner in which people within the business should treat each other and those outside the business. It is basically the answer to the questions, "What am I? Why am I this way?" It is a pattern of being. This concept is also called the firm's culture, memory, recipe, mental models, or frame of reference. People within the business use it to interpret what is happening around them. The terms most used to describe this idea are *mission, values,* and *culture.* The corporate culture shapes the way managers approach decision making, how they view the importance of hierarchy, and how they interrelate and act.

Like the other types of "vision," proponents of organizationally intended strategy formation claim that it is possible for this to be imposed from the top down. The techniques of Organizational Development (OD) are built on the assumption that it is possible for top management to install and change cultures in an intentional, predetermined manner, at least within limits. In this view, if the leaders of a company change what the company is trying to achieve, they can and should change the company culture to fit.

Belief that a company needs to have a pithily expressed business philosophy is reflected in the current recommendation that top managers write mission statements. Such statements are essentially attempts to encapsulate and communicate the chief tenets of the company's culture and to spread commitment to desired cultural norms throughout the organization. Examples of summarized business philosophy include that of IBM, which is said to be "service." The philosophy of People's Express was "People care." The culture of Marks and Spencer focuses on "quality."

Proponents of the organizationally intended mode of strategy formation state that successful companies have a strongly shared business philosophy and set of cultural values. Such culture and philosophy, they say, should be appropriate to the future state the firm is trying to reach and the kind of aspiration required for people to achieve it.

Those attempting cultural change and mission manufacturing activities are becoming increasingly disillusioned by the poor results achieved, however.[11] Such results are not surprising when one considers how cultures develop. Culture is a set of beliefs or assumptions that a group of people share concerning how to see things, how to interpret events, what it is valid to question, what answers are acceptable, how to behave toward others, and how to do things. The culture of a group of people develops as they associate with each other. The most important parts of it are unconscious, and they cannot be imposed from outside, even by top management.

Strongly Shared Norms

Sharing of group culture takes place at different levels. Norms may be shared at an apparent level or at an unconscious level. When we share norms at an apparent level, we conform superficially. We may wear the right clothes, perform the right acts, and say the right things without necessarily believing them. Such sharing is obvious but rather weak. We are aware of it, and we can relatively easily change what we are sharing.

When a group of people have lived or worked together for some time, however, they inevitably share norms at an unconscious level as well. These views on conduct, ways of performing, and modes of thinking are simply taken for granted. Group members do not have to display them to each other or communicate about them. They simply all follow them. When cultural sharing occurs at an unconscious level, it is strongly shared.

It takes a long time for such strong sharing to develop. It cannot be intentionally manufactured, installed, or changed by outsiders. It can emerge only from continued interaction between people in a group. Once culture is strongly shared, the power of conformity makes it extremely difficult to change. Only a very insensitive or a very courageous person tries to act contrary to the culture and still remain in the group.

The great advantage of strong sharing is that it cuts down on the need to communicate. It speeds up group action and creates powerful cohesion. The great disadvantage is that the assumptions that all in the group are then making are very rarely questioned. In turbulent times, these assumptions can quickly and disastrously become out of date. Strongly shared cultures inevitably block new learning and cut down on the variety of perspectives brought to bear on an issue. Well-established religious orders are prime examples of organizations in which cultural norms are strongly shared. Their ideologies do not allow for much change. This may be entirely appropriate for a religious order, but it is the opposite of what is required for a business operating in rapidly changing times.

Those presenting the organizationally intended mode of strategy formation recognize this and therefore prescribe a culture that loves change. But a strongly shared culture with a love of change is a contradiction in terms. When norms are strongly shared, they are shared at an unconscious level, and that, by definition, means a resistance to change. The more norms we strongly share, the more we resist changing them. If we strongly share a norm

encouraging change, we cannot then be strongly sharing other
norms because that would block change.

No group can operate effectively in the complete absence of
cultural sharing. Thus, in defining what norms it is appropriate to
share in a changing business it is helpful to distinguish between
what may be called performing norms and learning norms. Performing norms relate to what a group is doing together in carrying
out its day-to-day activities and how group members behave toward
each other as they do this. Learning norms relate to the way they
interpret what is going on around them, what it is permissible to
question, what answers it is acceptable to give, and generally how
they think about things. The sharing of both performing and learning norms at the apparent level is necessary for a group to work
effectively together—but this is weak sharing. Strong sharing, at the
unconscious level, of some important performing norms (such as
what constitutes quality or good customer service) may greatly improve the efficiency of the existing business. But strong sharing of
learning norms will always be harmful, and even strong sharing of
a few performing norms runs risks because such strong sharing
blocks complex learning.

Weakly Shared Norms

It was argued in Chapter Three that nonlinear feedback systems,
such as a business, must operate in conditions of bounded instability to be successful. The absence of strongly shared cultural norms
is one of the major characteristics of this dynamic in a business.
Such absence encourages the multiple perspectives required for innovative activity.

Weakly shared cultural norms also play another important
role in the dynamics of a successful business system. They provide
boundaries around sequences of choices. If all members of a group
strongly share the same culture, they may well pursue the same
sequence of choices for lengthy periods of time, with possibly disastrous consequences. If members of a group share nothing in terms
of culture, they will all move in widely different directions, leading
to explosive instability. If, however, cultural sharing takes a weak

form, the group will be able to work together but will not be likely to pursue the same sequence of choices for lengthy periods. Sooner or later some members will raise objections, leading to examination of what the group is doing. In this way, weak sharing provides important boundaries around instability while still allowing enough contention to break existing patterns of behavior and current perceptions.

Weakly shared cultural norms do weaken team cohesion. But does a successful work group need to be cohesive? During World War II, the behavior of bomb crews on missions to Germany was studied. Some of the crews were cohesive teams who liked each other and socialized together. Other crews were not cohesive in this sense. It turned out that the latter performed better because they focused on the task instead of socializing. Thus it seems that groups can work very effectively together without being cohesive. Mutual reliance on each other's contributions and some trust is all that is required. Cohesion creates social groups, not work groups.

The dynamic systems perspective leads to a view of culture as emergent. What a group comes to share in the way of culture and philosophy emerges from individual personal beliefs through a learning process that builds up over years.[12] And if the learning process is to continue, if a business is to be continually innovative, the emphasis should be on questioning the culture, not sharing it. A dynamic systems perspective points to the importance of encouraging countercultures in order to overcome powerful tendencies to conform and share cultures strongly.

A Dynamic View of Strategy Formation

The mental framework most managers today adopt is one in which there are, at least in principle, clear connections between causes and effects, so that it is possible to undertake actions in order to achieve predetermined outcomes. They think in terms of installing some form of systematic management process that will enable top managers to control the future development of the business.

The discovery that nonlinear feedback systems are capable of an additional form of behavior, bounded instability, opens up the possibility of a different model of strategy formation. In the chaotic dynamics that apply to this state, links between actions and their outcomes over the long term are lost in the detail of what actually happens. Managers therefore cannot form a vision of some future state toward which the business can be moved; the futures open to the system are too many, and the links between a future and the actions leading to it are too obscure. Chaotic dynamics lead us to see strategy as a direction into the future that emerges from what managers do. In chaotic conditions, strategy cannot be driven by prior intention. Instead, it represents the unintentional creation of order out of chaos.

The dynamic systems perspective thus leads managers to think in terms, not of the prior intention represented by objectives and visions, but of continuously developing agendas of issues, aspirations, challenges, and individual intentions. The key to emerging strategy is the effectiveness with which managers in an organization build and deal with such agendas of issues.

This perspective produces a different definition of intention in an organization. Instead of intention to secure something relatively known and fixed, it becomes intention to discover what, why, and how to achieve. Such intention arises not from what managers foresee but from what they have experienced and now understand. It is intention to be creative and deal with what comes, not intention to achieve some particular future state.

The dynamic systems perspective will alter the actions managers design in other important respects. The concern for developing common cultures and cohesive teams will be replaced with actions designed to promote different cultures in order to generate new perspectives while still placing boundaries around sequences of choices.

When we interpret the strategy formation process from the dynamic systems perspective, we think about strategies in a different way. The new frame of reference leads us to ask how we can intend, not the specific pattern of action that is a strategy, but the effective learning and political behavior that makes it possible for a pattern to emerge. We see emergence as a process by means of which the business system as a whole can create order out of chaos. As groups, managers reach periodic consensus about and commitment to a particular response to a specific open-ended issue. That response may be the start of an innovation, a new strategic direction. It is not from a preordained central vision but from the ongoing, spontaneous, and self-organizing processes of learning and political interaction that patterns in long-term sequences of actions—that is, the strategies of the business—emerge.

7

Strategic Control: Managing the Boundary Between Plans and Change

Managers today approach the problem of control from two different angles. On the one hand, they see control as a planning and monitoring activity that requires clear hierarchies of managers with well-defined roles, as well as rules, regulations, and procedures governing the allocation of authority and responsibility for achieving objectives. On the other hand, they see control as ideological in nature. Control in this form is exercised through shared beliefs in a vision and a common set of values or culture. Control by planning is an essentially structural approach, with the advantage of clarity but the disadvantage of inflexbility. Control by ideology is an essentially behavioral approach, with the advantage of flexibility but the disadvantage of being less governable from the center. In practice, managers generally adopt some combination of these two approaches.

Although they are different in many respects, both of these forms of control nonetheless have the same aim and are based on the same unquestioned assumptions. The aim of both the structural and the ideological forms of control is to secure regularity in the pattern of behavior of the business system as a whole and help it adapt to its environment—in other words, to create an organization in stable equilibrium. In both cases, control is implemented through negative feedback loops that keep the organization moving toward some intentionally predetermined future point. Both the structural and the ideological forms of control are based on the assumption that there are reasonably close links between causes and their effects, between actions and their outcomes. Both approaches assume that the same control philosophy can be applied to the short-term and the long-term futures facing the business. Strategic control is not seen as conceptually different from day-to-day control; the former is simply a less precise version of the latter.

Both views of control are also alike in that they picture some individual or small group of individuals as being in control of the behavior of the business system and the outcomes of that behavior over both the short and the long term. Those at the top set the objectives and establish the rules and hierarchies, formulate the vision and define the culture, or both. In short, systems for both short-term and strategic control are to be centrally installed and directed in some sense.

However, when we view the behavior of a business organization from a dynamic systems perspective, we relegate today's received wisdom on the nature of control to the short-term control of a business. We realize that strategic or long-term control must be understood in completely different terms. This chapter will argue that, since the long-term future of a dynamic system is unknowable because cause-and-effect links are lost in the detail of what happens, the long-term control of a business has to take a form different from that pictured by the received wisdom. These forms are political interaction and complex learning. When performed effectively, these activities do produce controlled behavior, even though no individual is in control of them. They produce and depend upon bounded instability and nonequilibrium states, not stability and equilibrium. They are implemented by amplifying feedback that spreads new perspectives through an organization. They are concerned with patterns in action, or strategies, that are irregular rather than regular because the strategies represent innovative breaks with the past. They are essentially self-organizing forms of control, and those at the top of the organization contribute to these forms of control indirectly, by creating a climate in which complex learning and healthy political interaction can thrive. Political interaction and complex learning are the only forms of control suitable for handling open-ended change, which dominates the long-term future of a business.

The dynamic systems view shows overall control of a business to be the simultaneous application of diametrically opposed forms of behavior. Planning and ideological forms of control, with their relatively inflexible hierarchies and compliant behavior, are essential for effective management of the existing business from day to day. At the same time, strategic control as self-organizing politics and learning must be practiced if the business is to develop new direction. This form of control requires the opposite of compliance; indeed, it actually threatens existing day-to-day activities because it generates questioning and contention. Control in total terms is the continual orchestration of the tensions created by the need to apply both short-interval and strategic forms of control, by the opposing pulls of stability and instability.

The need for these two completely different forms of control arises because a business simultaneously faces completely different types of changing situations: those involving closed change or contained change, and those involving open-ended change. This chapter will examine all three kinds of situation in detail. It will then consider how and why different forms of control apply to these different kinds of change situations.

Three Kinds of Change

Management is fundamentally about handling change. How managers do this has to depend upon the principal characteristics of that change, if their actions are to be effective. What, then, are the principal characteristics or kinds of change generated by dynamic systems?

The current state of a dynamic system is a record of everything that has happened to it and everything that the actors or components within it have done in the past. When the system is far from equilibrium, its history is important and will have major effects on what happens to the system in the future. Managers quite clearly recognize this. At the start of every consultancy assignment I have been on, the client managers recount the history of their organization as a way of explaining its current situation. Managers and consultants alike recognize that they cannot understand what to do next until they have established some understanding of what has happened. For this reason, board and top executive meetings are often dominated by accounts of what has happened.

Closed Change

When we look back at the history of a business, some sequences of events can be recounted clearly, in a manner that commands the widespread agreement of all the managers involved. Everyone agrees on what happened, why it happened, what the consequences were, and how such a sequence of events and actions are likely to affect the future course of the business. We can call these situations of closed change.

The principal features of closed change are that the consequences of events are clearly understandable in their past form and accurately predictable in their future form. These features apply because the events and actions generating the consequences have already occurred and causality is clear cut. Such situations predominate in the normal, continuing operation of an existing business. For example, consider a business that supplies popular records and tapes to the teenage market. Managers in that business are able to say with some precision how the number of customers in that market has changed over the past. They can also say how the number will change for the next fifteen years or so, since those customers already exist; statistics on the number of births in each of the past fifteen years are available. Furthermore, the managers can establish fairly clear-cut relationships between the number of customers and the number of records and tapes they have bought. This will help to indicate how many they will buy.

Closed change is depicted in Figure 7.1 as the shaded area under curve A. This curve shows how a sequence of actions and events began at some point in the past (time t_{-1} on the horizontal axis), how the consequences developed to the present (t_0), and how they will proceed into the future.

Contained Change

Other sequences of events and actions flowing from the past are less clear cut. Here we find that we are able to say only what probably

Figure 7.1. Situations of Change Generated by Past Events and Actions.

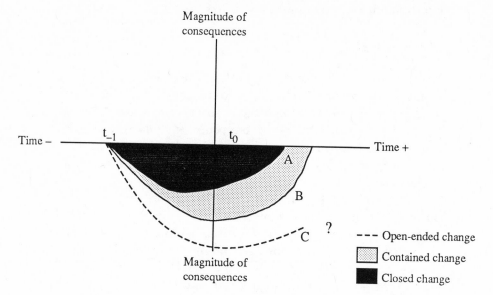

happened, why it probably happened, and what its probable consequences were. The impact of such a sequence of events upon the future must similarly be qualified by probability statements. For example, the supplier of records and tapes will find it harder to explain why particular kinds of records and tapes sold better than others or to forecast what kinds of tapes and records will sell better in the future. Still, market research, life-style studies, and statistical projections will allow reasonably helpful forecasts to be made for at least the short term. Causality in these situations is approximate or statistical; it takes the form of probability statements. We can call this kind of change contained. It is represented in Figure 7.1 as the hatched area under curve B.

Open-ended Change

There are yet other sequences of events and actions arising from the past and continuing to affect the future for which no explanation commands anything like widespread acceptance by those involved. The company supplying records and tapes may have decided in the

past to diversify into video film distribution by acquiring another .
company already in that business, but it now finds that this acquisition is unprofitable. The managers involved could well subscribe to
conflicting explanations of why this is so. For example, some may
claim that the market for video films is too competitive, others that
the diversification was a wrong move because it meant operating in
a different market with which they were not sufficiently familiar,
and still others that the unprofitability is due to a temporary decline
in demand and that the market will pick up in the future. Other
explanations may ascribe the problem to poor management of the
acquisition, to a failure to integrate it properly into the business,
or to a clash of cultures between the two businesses. What that team
of managers do next to deal with this present situation obviously
depends upon the explanation of past failure they eventually agree
on—if they do.

The change in this kind of situation may be called open
ended. Here we do not know with any clarity what caused the
change or what all its consequences were or will be. It is depicted
in Figure 7.1 as the blank area under the dotted curve, C. That curve
ends with a question mark because the managers do not know what
the consequences of this kind of sequence of events and actions will
be in the future.

Change and the Future

As they stand in the here and now, at time t_0 in Figure 7.1, managers
face three different kinds of changing situation arising from sequences of events and actions that have already occurred. There are
also sequences of events and actions that are starting up now, in the
present. Some of these will be situations of closed change, such as
an existing customer placing a much larger order for an existing
product line. Some sequences of events and actions will be situations of contained change, such as a new customer placing orders
for a modified range of products. And others will be situations of
open-ended change, such as setting up a new company branch in
Poland.

Yet other sequences of events and actions will be initiated at
future points. These sequences also will be either closed, contained,

or open ended. Figure 7.1 is completed in Figure 7.2 by the addition
of curves representing these present and future consequences. (The
vertical axis measures the magnitude of the consequences, without
distinguishing between negative and positive effects. The diagram
is drawn this way simply for visual clarity.)

The point the diagram makes is this. As they stand in the
present, managers in any company face a spectrum of changing
situations with beginnings in every time frame, from the past
through the present to the future. At each point, that spectrum
stretches from predictable closed change, through statistically predictable contained change, into unknowable open-ended change.
The past and the short-term future are dominated by closed and
contained change, but the long-term future is open ended.

This pattern of change situations is a consequence of the
dynamics of the business system. When dynamics are chaotic, small
changes escalate and self-reinforcing circles develop, making it totally impossible to predict the specific long-term future consequences of sequences of events and actions. In this sense the long-
term future of the system is inherently unknowable. But because it

Figure 7.2. Situations of Change in the Present and Future.

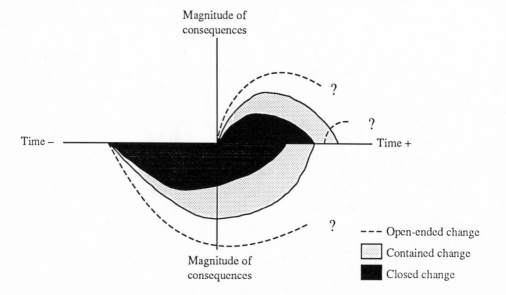

takes time for escalation to occur, it is possible to forecast the short-term future of the system. Thus, as we stand in the present we face a short-term future that we can largely foresee and a long-term future that we can know nothing specific about. Of course, when we reach that long-term point, we will find it to be a mixture of consequences that we can then understand and consequences that we cannot. But in the meantime, in the present, we have to decide and act knowing absolutely nothing in specific terms about those long-term consequences.

Closed and contained change relate to developments that have short-term consequences. To the extent that short-term consequences are more or less repetitions of what has happened before, it is practically useful to apply probability concepts and statistical techniques to specify their consequences. Open-ended change, however, is unique and has never happened in that specific form before. Measures of probability therefore have no practical use in making decisions about open-ended changes. Simulating the future of the business, or building scenarios of its possible futures, will not provide forecasts of the likely range of outcomes of such changes; these exercises can provide only learning or practice to get a feel for the kinds of future patterns that may develop.

Managers cannot choose to focus on one kind of change or another if they wish to survive. A business must simultaneously deal with all three forms. Because open-ended change is qualitatively different from closed and contained change, however, it will have to be dealt with in a completely different way.

Change and Behavior

Because reasonably clear-cut links can be established between causes and effects in situations involving closed or contained change, such situations have consequences that can be forecast to a reasonably useful degree of accuracy. This means that the problems and opportunities facing managers in these situations also are reasonably clear. Any difficulties lie in finding answers, not in identifying the questions to ask. Such situations are not characterized by ambiguity, and competent managers do not therefore respond to them in an equivocal manner. If managers conflict in such a situation, they probably can settle the conflict by rational argument. Failing that, the application of power as authority derived from the clear rules and structures of the organization can be applied to settle differences, or bargains of one sort or another can be used to resolve the conflict. People by and large know what they are doing in closed and contained situations. Indeed, they usually have largely decided what to do before such a change occurs. The behavior of groups of people and the shared models they use to design their actions therefore are all understandable and reasonably predictable in these kinds of situations.

When managers confront open-ended change, however, the situation is completely different in every respect. They are now faced with actions and events (past, present, or future) that have unknowable—not merely currently unknown—consequences. Links between cause and effect are lost in the detail of those events because small changes escalate and self-reinforcing circles appear. The key difficulty becomes that of identifying what the problems and opportunities are, deciding what questions to ask, rather than finding answers. The situation is ambiguous, and the responses of managers to it are equivocal. In these uniquely new situations, old shared mental models showing how to design actions do not work; new mental models have to be developed and shared before anything can happen. Conflict about how to interpret what is going on and how to design actions to deal with it becomes commonplace and inevitable. Indeed, it is a vital part of developing new mental models. Predetermined rules and authority structures become useless as effective means of settling the conflicts because these things presuppose that someone has made up his or her mind and knows what to do.

The unpredictability of specific events within fuzzy categories, which is the hallmark of open-ended change, leads to ambiguity and confusion. Although human minds are well equipped to deal with such situations, the situations remain difficult because they require developing new mental models through analogical reasoning. That difficulty is magnified many times when a new mental model must come to be shared by a number of people in the management team before they can take joint action. The manner in which the team members interact with each other then becomes a vital part of the decision-making process they employ. We cannot understand what they decide to do without understanding the impact of their personalities and the impact of group dynamics. In this kind of situation, people typically feel insecure and become anxious, with the result that their group dynamics become much more complex and may often become bizarre. There is a strong tendency to apply inappropriate mental models to the learning process.

Characteristics of Controlled Behavior

Before we consider what forms of control apply to different kinds of change, we need to describe what we mean by controlled behavior. Controlled behavior has some overall coherence or pattern; that is, it is internally connected and constrained. It is the opposite of haphazard, unconnected thinking and acting without any pattern, or unconstrained explosively unstable behavior.

Connectedness

For behavior to be connected there has to be a feedback loop joining the following activities: discovering what is going on or changing; making conscious or unconscious choices to respond to, or provoke, changes; acting upon those choices; and discovering what the consequences of those actions are, in order to make further choices and take further actions. These elements of discovery, choice, and action must be connected in the sense that choice is based on what is discovered, action flows from choice, and the consequences of action are discovered so as to influence the next choice. People may go around this loop rapidly or slowly; they may do so in a deliberate, analytical way or in an automatic, unconscious way. No matter how they do it, the connections must be there if behavior is to be controlled.

Sometimes this feedback connection breaks down, and human behavior becomes uncontrolled. Two people may argue fiercely but still be controlled, if each consciously or unconsciously discovers the reaction of the other to a statement (in other words, listens to the other) and then makes the next statement in the light of that discovery. If, however, each person simply makes a series of statements without hearing or understanding the other, the result is an uncontrolled argument that is either haphazard and meaningless or explodes into a quarrel.

All controlled behavior must follow this connected feedback loop, but the elements of that loop (discovery, choice, and action) may be defined in different ways. Indeed, they must be defined in different ways in situations of closed or contained change and situations of open-ended change because those kinds of situations are so different. In closed and contained change, the feedback can be negative, precise, and analytical, but in open-ended situations, it must be amplifying, loose, and political.

Constraint

In addition to connected feedback, control requires the presence of some form of constraint that prevents behavior from becoming explosively unstable. We normally see that constraint in an organization as being provided by some form of shared organizational intention. It may be an end point all are striving for; it may be a path all agree to follow; it may be a set of rules all agree (or are compelled) to obey. This form of constraint requires central direction and mechanisms for securing agreement or acceptance. It usually is implemented by negative feedback. But we do not have to define constraint in this way, and indeed in situations of open-ended change we cannot. In open-ended situations, constraint is provided by the need to secure and sustain the support of others, as well as the need to persuade and convince others of a point of view. Constraint cannot be imposed in open-ended situations; it is a self-organizing property of the system.

Pattern

Controlled behavior must also have a third characteristic: pattern. Negative feedback in a system produces a regular and therefore repetitive pattern of actions and consequences. But controlled behavior can also take the form of irregular patterns. For example, the weather system produces controlled behavior, yet weather patterns are irregular. Controlled business behavior in open-ended situations also produces irregular rather than regular patterns.

Control in Situations of Closed or Contained Change

The elements of the feedback control loop (discovery, choice, and action) can be defined precisely, and the loop can be driven by negative feedback to produce regular patterns in action, only when the changes in a situation are closed or contained. In closed or contained situations, the consequences of change are predictable; there is a clear link between cause and effect. Control in these situations therefore can be exerted through planning or ideology, which require such predictability. These forms of control are appropriate for the short term of a business, which is dominated by situations of closed or contained change.

Planning

In control by planning, behavior is connected in that there are clearly laid out steps from discovery as formal, analytical scanning of the environment; to choice as objective setting and plan formation; to action as plan implementation; and then back through formal monitoring to discovery again. Here, behavior is constrained by organizational intention relating to objectives and planned routes to them. The pattern of action produced is regular movement toward the objective. This control loop is depicted in Figure 7.3.

Ideology

In the ideological model of control, the ideology consists of an overarching organizational vision or intention that all are inspired to follow, accompanied by the strong sharing of core cultural values throughout the organization. Discovery, choice, and action are connected by a feedback loop in which the connections run from discovery as informal listening and observation; to choice as a vision; to action as trial-and-error experiments; and back to discovery again through learning about the outcomes of action.

Behavior in this form of control is constrained by the ideology itself and by the criteria for trial-and-error action. The ideology provides some of these criteria. Others are provided by the principle of focus, which states that trial actions should constitute a logically

Figure 7.3. Control by Planning in Closed or Contained Situations.

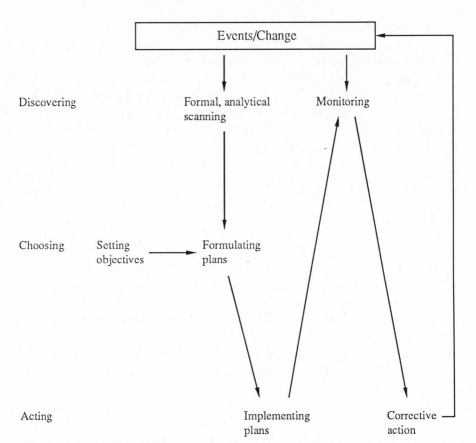

incremental move from the existing core business. This control loop is depicted in Figure 7.4.

This form of control and development is fundamental to the popular approach to success prescribed by writers such as Tom Peters.[1] He presses managers to form a vision—a picture of a future state—and then reach that vision by undertaking hectic trial-and-error actions that satisfy criteria set by shared values and logical connection to the existing business. But, what conditions need to prevail if a process of trial-and-error action according to given criteria is dependably to lead to a vision decided in advance of the ac-

**Figure 7.4. Control by Vision and Ideology in Closed or
Contained Situations.**

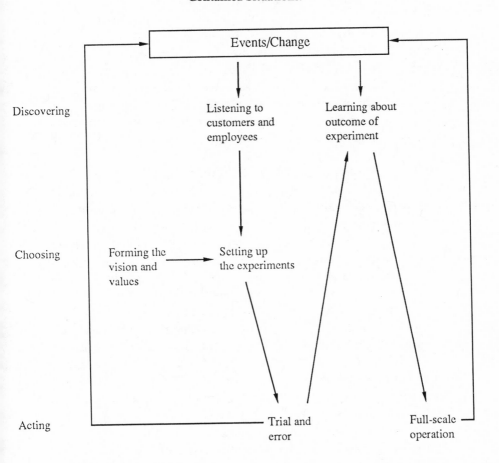

tion? In other words, what is it necessary to assume about the nature of an organization and its environment in order to make it sensible to prescribe this form of control and development?

The answer to this question is provided by cybernetics (the science of control), in particular by what is called Ashby's law of "Requisite Variety."[2] This law states that a system will remain stable if its control, or regulator, displays the same level of variety as the environment in which the control is to be exerted. The variety of the environment is simply the number of changes, or random shocks, it generates, and the variety of the regulator in a system is simply the number of responses it can make to those changes or shocks. This is a rather elaborate way of saying that the faster the environment changes, the faster the system has to respond to stay stable. What is not so obvious, however, is the mechanism that is proposed for responding. Ashby's law says that it is enough to have the same number of responses as environmental shocks, not that each response to each shock has to be the right one. In other words, the mechanism is trial and error, and all that is necessary is to get the level or speed of trial and error right. What is the justification for this?

The justification is the law of large numbers, or probability. If large numbers of random shocks, or unforeseeable changes, keep hitting a system and if that system undertakes large numbers of basically random small trial actions in response, then obviously only some random actions will match some of the random shocks in the sense of being appropriate responses. Most will not, but because of the large numbers involved, the inappropriate responses will tend to cancel each other out—the laws of large numbers. Provided that a system acts fast enough, it will maintain stability and move toward its goal—but only if shocks and responses are closely similar, for example, repetitive events of the kind we get when we toss a coin, where the result always is either heads or tails. It is only with large numbers of repetitive events that we can rely on the canceling out of mismatches between random shocks and random actions because it is only then that the law of large numbers works.

When a dynamic system operates in conditions of bounded instability, however, as a business does in the long term, no specific event is ever repeated in exactly the same way. The probability of any specific event occurring is therefore infinitely small. Each specific event is unique, falling only into general qualitative categories in which items bear a family resemblance to each other. A business does not typically get a large number of chances to repeat events that bear a family resemblance close enough to apply probability in even an approximate way. Furthermore, if some tiny shock is not met with exactly the right response, the mismatch could escalate, with completely unpredictable results in a dynamic system.

Under these circumstances, there is no guarantee that trial-

and-error mismatches with random environmental shocks will cancel out. Large numbers of random actions, even within boundaries set by logical connection with the existing business and core values, cannot be relied upon as a search technique that will take the business to its intended vision. The ideological form of control requires a causal connection between the vision and the actions required to realize it. It can therefore be applied only in situations of closed and contained change, and attempts to apply it in other situations are based on unquestioned assumptions that on deeper reflection clearly do not apply to businesses.

Control in Situations of Open-ended Change

States of stable equilibrium are often desirable. When the human heart moves away from stable equilibrium into chaos, the result is a heart attack. We do not want a country's electricity system to operate in any state other than stable equilibrium. Most of us desire to see some human systems, too, remain stable. Most do not want religious organizations, for example, to display the bounded instability that may lead them to be innovative.

Business organizations, however, are human feedback systems that must innovate continually if they are to survive. To do so, as has been explained, they have to operate away from equilibrium in the area of bounded instability. Complex learning and political interaction are the only forms of control capable of operating in this area and of dealing with situations of open-ended change. They are therefore the only forms appropriate to long-term business development, which is dominated by this kind of change. These forms of control are creative and not in equilibrium. They were described in detail in Chapter Four.

Since a successful business system is one in which (at least in the long term) relation to continuing predetermined and shared intention is impossible, patterns in action are essentially irregular, and relationships with the environment are creatively interactive, there can be no template against which to measure control. Long-term control through damping feedback therefore is impossible. Instead, control in the forms of learning and political interaction is implemented by amplifying feedback that operates within boundaries. A business system properly develops by amplifying small changes, as when individuals fasten onto some issue, build support for their views about it, and so possibly turn it into a new direction for the company.

Although learning and political action produce controlled behavior, no individual or small group controls them. Top management, however, exerts an influence on these forms of control that is just as important as the influence it exerts through plans and visions; the area of influence is simply different. Instead of influencing through fixing intentions and establishing predetermined rules to yield an outcome—none of which can be done in a situation of open-ended change—top management exerts its influence by operating on the boundary conditions surrounding the learning process in the organizations, that is, the context within which it occurs. In this way it determines whether learning occurs at all, how widespread that learning is, and what quality is displays. Those boundary conditions have to do with the manner in which power is used, the group dynamics it provokes, the culture of the group, and the time pressures it faces. This concept of boundary conditions, or context, is discussed in Chapter Eight, and Chapter Nine discusses how managers may intervene to influence the boundary conditions.

Chaotic Behavior as Controlled Behavior

Control exerted by learning and political interaction amplifies rather than damps, but it amplifies within boundaries. Both these forms of control spread issues and perspectives through an organization, challenging existing patterns and therefore destabilizing, but that instability is constrained. Learning and political interaction, in fact, produce behavior that is just as coherent and controlled as that produced by planning and vision fulfillment.

Like the forms of control that lead to stable equilibrium, control through learning and political interaction produces behavior that is connected, constrained, and patterned. The connections in the amplifying feedback loop for these kinds of control were pictured in Figure 4.1, which appeared in Chapter Four. That figure should be compared with Figure 7.3 in this chapter. Like the loop for planning, the loop for learning and political interaction connects discovery, choice, and action. However, the elements of the loop for learning and political interaction cannot be defined as precisely as those in the planning loop, and they have to be defined in a different way as the two diagrams make clear. The constraint and the pattern in the behavior produced by learning and political interaction are discussed below.

It is important to note that central, shared intention is not an essential requirement for controlled behavior. We can intend explosive instability, which is not controlled. On the other hand, behavior may be chaotic, without central shared intention, and yet be controlled. Predictability and stability also are not essential requirements for control. Explosive instability follows a perfectly predictable course, yet it is not controlled. Chaotic behavior, by contrast, is unpredictable and unstable but still controlled.

Learning as Control

People learning in a group are displaying controlled behavior. Connections run from the discovery by individuals of small changes, anomalies, and ambiguities; to choice arising out of reflection, contention, and dialogue concerning the issues being discovered; to exploratory action; and back to discovery again as the processes of choice and the outcomes of exploratory actions provide further prompts to individual discoveries. Here behavior is constrained partly by individual differences in culture and perceptions and by disagreements that prevent a single view from dominating. Behavior is also partly constrained by the shared views that groups working together come to acquire, yet must constantly question if they are to learn. Constraint, then, is a consequence of the tension between sharing and difference. The extremes of sharing and difference both remove the constraints and lead to uncontrolled behavior. There are also patterns in the behavior of people learning together in a group. These are irregular categories of behavior—archetypes. For example, in one pattern the learning group displays dependent behavior in one of its members and in another pattern they may avoid the learning risk or fight with each other.

Politics as Control

People interacting politically are also displaying controlled behavior. Connection runs from discovery as the formation of individual and subunit issues; to choice as the building of support through persuasion and negotiation, the application of power; to action; and back to discovery again as action generates yet other issues. Behavior is constrained by the unequal distribution of power, by the existence of hierarchy, and by the need to sustain sufficient support for views about issues and actions to be taken in regard to them. Political interaction also generates irregular but recognizable patterns in behavior depending on the manner in which power is used. For example, continued exertion of authority may generate patterns of compliance or rebellion.

An example of political activity as a form of control is provided by the removal of Prime Minister Thatcher from office in the United Kingdom in 1991. This powerful figure gradually lost support because of her position on the issues of the United Kingdom's relationship with the European Economic Community and of the poll tax. Opposition groups formed covertly. One of these crystallized around Heseltine and became overt. A somewhat ambiguous support group formed around Thatcher, but within it there were factions, one supporting Major as an alternative and another supporting Hurd. On the first ballot Thatcher did not secure enough votes, by a very small margin. At first she intended to go to a second ballot, but then, apparently because of the advice of a small number of people, she withdrew. Major won on the second ballot.

Here the outcome was unpredictable—events unfolded—yet hindsight revealed a pattern in the way coalitions formed and shifted; behavior was contained and connected. No one centrally directed the formation of the factions and coalitions that determined the final result. The process was not driven by a plan or a shared culture; on the contrary, differences in views and values were the drivers. Those involved were amplifying and spreading views in a destabilizing manner. A small difference from the required vote in the first ballot had escalating consequences. Throughout, however, behavior was constrained by the need to sustain support and thus was controlled, even though no individual was controlling it.

Much the same process occurs when a business deals with open-ended issues. It is not as obvious in that case because the process is not played out on a media stage. It therefore often is not examined or even perceived to be a form of control. The kind of control represented by political interaction nonetheless is vital to the long-term development of an innovative business.

Using Opposite Forms of Control Simultaneously

Any business faces a spectrum of changing situations. Over the short term, the consequences of changes created by and affecting the system are to some useful extent predictable. Change in such situations is usually closed or contained. Control through planning or ideology works perfectly well in these situations. Indeed, managers who understand the chaotic dynamics of a successful business will place a good deal of emphasis on tight short-interval control because it provides an important element of stability to a business that has to operate in conditions under which the long-term future is unknowable. They also will emphasize short-interval control because it automates responses to short-term consequences of change and thus leaves more time to attend to the challenging, open-ended changes that affect the long term. Finally, such managers will emphasize short-interval control because this kind of control provides the means consistently to deliver low-cost, high-quality, and appropriate service levels.

At the same time, managers of successful companies will apply other forms of control—namely, control through complex learning and political interaction—to deal with the situations of open-ended change that dominates a business's long term. They will recognize that in situations of open-ended change one cannot specify an intention and then identify a limited number of events and actions that will lead to fulfillment of that intention because links between cause and effect are lost in the complexity of unfolding events. Forms of control that require prior, overarching organizational intention therefore are inappropriate to such situations. Managers cannot rely upon setting predetermined rules and routes for individuals within the organization to follow, against which conduct can be monitored. They cannot use negative or damping feedback to sustain equilibrium.

This does not mean that there can be no form of strategic control, however. Rather, it means that managers have to think about control in a more general sense. The behavior of a business organization as a whole may be controlled, even though no agent within or outside it is able to control, in the sense of determining, the specific outcomes of its behavior. The system can control itself in a self-organizing way if the context is right.

Managers of successful companies will recognize that open-ended change removes all the conditions required for the practice of the planning and ideological modes of control and development. They therefore will abandon all attempts at long-term planning and envisioning. Instead, they will rely on complex learning and political interaction in groups to produce not only control but emergent intention, strategy, culture, and business philosophy. They will accept the inevitable unpredictability and irregularity of the innovative or creative approach. This advice to abandon long-term planning is not advice to abandon all concern with the long term. Instead, it is a recommendation to search for realistic modes of maintaining and coping with bounded instability and open-ended change.

The art of management is the ability both to alternate between very different forms of control at different points in time and to ensure that these different forms are being applied in different parts of the organization at the same point in time. Managers need to choose appropriate forms of control for handling both short-term and long-term changes and, especially, to identify more effective frameworks within which to design actions to deal with the open-ended changes that the long-term future of a business brings.

8

Participation, Hierarchy, and Stability: Finding the Middle Ground

Over the past decade there has been growing concern about the ability of rigid organizational hierarchies to cope with increasingly complex and turbulent business conditions. That concern has led to more and more top management interest in installing "flexible organizational structures" and mounting "culture change" programs to empower people throughout an organization. The aim of both the restructuring and the culture change is the same: to free employees and those below the top in the management hierarchy from instructions and controls and to allow them to make decisions themselves. It is believed that this approach will make organizations more responsive to the marketplace, encourage people to be more innovative, reduce administration costs by cutting out layers of management, and improve collaboration by making it easier for people to communicate horizontally from one business function or unit to another.

At first sight, these ideas seem to be entirely consistent with the dynamic systems perspective of management that has been developed in previous chapters. From that perspective, innovative strategic directions can emerge only if managers at many levels interact politically and engage in complex learning together in a spontaneous manner; that is, if they self-organize. That, surely, is flexibility and empowerment.

On more careful reflection, however, it becomes clear that currently popular ideas about flexible structures and empowerment

169

of individuals are substantially at odds with a dynamic systems perspective. This is so for two reasons. First, a dynamic systems perspective leads us to emphasize the importance of strong hierarchies for the tight short-term control of a business. Currently popular prescriptions for flexible structures and empowered people intentionally weaken the hierarchy and thereby destroy the short-term control system. Second, the dynamic systems perspective shows that it is vital to sustain the paradox of simultaneous flexibility and control, whereas currently popular ideas on the flexible organization seek to resolve that paradox by choosing a balance that favors flexibility. In the dynamic systems concept, successful managers choose both strong hierarchies for short-term control and self-organizing processes of political interaction and learning out of which new long-term direction may emerge. In the flexible organization concept, however, managers face the choice between tight short-term control and flexibility through so-called "self-managing" teams (dispersed power, widespread participation, wide spans of control, supportive supervision), and they are advised to make a choice that favors the latter. Thus it is clear that managers designing their actions according to a mental model based on the concept of dynamic systems will behave very differently from those operating according to the model of the flexible organization.

This chapter considers these two significant differences in more detail. In so doing, it also explains the distinction between self-organizing processes and "self-managing teams."

Flexible Organizations and Short-Interval Control

The first recommendation for the flexible organization is that a flexible structure be installed. As it is used in the current debate, the term *flexible structure* usually has one of two meanings. One definition refers to a simple, highly decentralized structure in which decision-making authority and control over resources are devolved. People in this structure work in small units close to the marketplace, run by managers who have authority to respond to changes in that marketplace.[1] The price of this kind of flexible structure is loss of synergy and collaboration among parts of the organization.

Those who regard this as too high a price to pay prefer the second definition.

The second definition of *flexible structure* is an organizational structure that brings people together across functional and business unit boundaries.[2] Such a structure takes the form either of a matrix, in which most people have reporting lines to more than one superior, or of a formal network, in which the horizontal as well as the vertical links between one manager and another are formally specified. Both of these structures are inevitably complex, and working in them is more difficult than working in simpler, decentralized ones. Some believe, however, that this drawback is outweighed by the benefits of cross-fertilization and the challenge that the more difficult structures represent.

Both definitions of flexible structure include the idea of the "flat" structure reached through what is called delayering—cutting out layers of middle managers to improve vertical communication and widening spans of control so that the managerial role becomes more one of coaching or mentoring than of directing or controlling. Proponents of delayering recognize that this process spreads the middle management resource rather thinly, but they see this as a source of challenge rather than a disadvantage. Because the environment is so complex and changes so rapidly, supporters of delayering say, everyone in the organization needs to take an interest in everything. They believe that clear role and job definitions "put people in boxes" and cut down on their range of perceptions and thus actions. Both definitions of a flexible structure therefore specify overlapping roles and loose job definitions. Both definitions also advise managers to tear up the rule books and free people to cope with the environment.

In addition to installing flexible structure, the flexible organization concept recommends empowering people to act. Empowerment here means establishing widespread participation in decision making and dispersing power, including power to allocate resources, throughout the organization.[3] Empowerment includes encouraging employees to contribute ideas; setting up small teams of employees to make and implement the decisions necessary to redesign their jobs; and involving employees in decisions that affect the whole organization. The emphasis is on teamwork and team problem solving. Supervisors and managers, in this view, support rather than direct.

These prescriptions for a flexible organization are always coupled with insistence on two features designed to keep the organization in a state of stable consensus. The first feature is strongly shared vision and values, and the second is tight short-term financial control. These features establish the climate in which the self-managing teams are to function. Freedom to act combined with the demands for consensus and close financial monitoring is said to be a paradox summed up in the phrase "loose-tight" control.

A flexible organization is supposed to consist of a particular constellation of self-managing teams that are a permanent part of a centrally installed structure. Self-managing teams have formally specified, permanent leaders who are either appointed or elected. Team members also are formally appointed and permanent. The formally defined role of the leaders is to be supportive. The members' roles are defined by loose job descriptions and the right to make suggestions and participate in what is probably meant to be democratic decision making. Rules about what decisions they are to participate in and how are also formally established when the teams are set up.

When one considers what is necessary for the operation of an effective short-interval control system, however, it becomes clear that "loose-tight" control is not a paradox but a logical inconsistency. The essence of tight short-interval control is a clear allocation of responsibility for carrying out predetermined tasks that have reasonably predictable results to which rewards are tied. We cannot allocate clear responsibility for predetermined tasks unless those tasks are clearly defined. Loose role and job definitions accompanied by flexible hierarchies and organizational structures therefore are completely incompatible with tight short-interval control. Tight short-term control is essentially management by rules and manuals. Tearing these up simply destroys the system. The essence of this form of control is frequent and regular formal review and reporting. The operation of an effective short-interval control system therefore requires managers to collect and present information, to attend review meetings, and to carry out corrective action promptly. If the stripping out of layers of middle managers is carried too far, it will damage the ability to carry out tight short-interval control.

Widespread participation in decision making and the dispersal of power to allocate resources are also incompatible with tight short-interval control. The short-term control system is essentially a top-down one in which top management sets targets, after some negotiation with those lower down, and retains the power to allocate resources. It is through power to allocate resources that the top maintains short-term control and stability. In the short term, resources are allocated under predictable circumstances for predetermined purposes only.

Flexible organizations and tight short-interval control are thus completely incompatible. The choice here is an "either/or" one: either an organization has clear hierarchies with clear job definitions and power increasing markedly as one moves up the hierarchy, or it has much diminished short-term financial control. The dynamic systems model developed in earlier chapters makes the choice quite clearly in favor of hierarchies and short-term control, thereby rejecting the idea of a comprehensive structure of self-managing teams.

To be sure, some might say that some degree of effectiveness in short-interval control could well be worth sacrificing if doing so led to better decision making and strategy formation. But does it?

Flexible Organizations and Decision Making

On the face of it, widespread participation in decision making and more equally shared power should lead to more people detecting changes that occur in the environment and taking trial actions to deal with the uncertainty those changes provoke. However, some interesting studies have been carried out on the decision-making process in organizations that have flexible structures of the kind we have been talking about. These studies suggest that widespread participation in fact inhibits effective decision making.[4]

Universities and some state bodies have flat, complex matrix structures; unclear hierarchies; very loose job definitions; widespread participation in decision making; and a fairly equal distribution of power. Studies of such organizations have found that their decision-making processes take what has been called a "garbage can" form. Because of the complex matrix structure, large numbers of people can concern themselves with just about any issue, which they can raise at just about any decision-making forum. Decision-making forums then take the form of a "garbage can" into which issues, problems, and solutions tend to be thrown in a somewhat haphazard manner. Added to this, the participation of people in such forums tends to be fluid, with different people attending at different times because there are few rules requiring regular attendance. What issues are attended to and how they are resolved depends upon which group members are present, how interested they are in the issue, what other issues are attracting their attention, and what other work pressures are distracting them. In these circumstances, decisions emerge almost by chance. Since power is widely distributed, the ability to use the political system of the organization to shape the agenda of issues and give greater coherence to the decision-making process is severely limited. Widely distributed power also means that even when issues survive on the agenda long enough to be the subjects of decisions, those decisions often will not be implemented. (The process of handling strategic issue agendas described in Chapter Four sounds similar to what has just been described. A critical difference, however, lies in the boundaries around the two processes—in particular in the way power is distributed. This difference will be discussed later in this chapter.)

To be sure, the situation of the universities and other bodies surveyed in these studies differs in several important respects from the flexible organization concept discussed earlier. First, universities tend not to have much in the way of overall visions or strongly shared cultures. They usually have a few widely shared beliefs about academic freedom and fairness, but they are likely to contain many different cultures in, for example, different academic disciplines. Furthermore, the tasks carried out at universities have what might be called an uncertain technology. For example, it is not at all clear what constitutes good teaching. The experts carrying out the tasks therefore have to be allowed a considerable level of personal freedom of judgment. The result of this combination of most aspects of the flexible organization with a lack of shared vision and culture and uncertain task technology is that very little organizational strategy is formed. As Mintzberg and Waters write,

> Unconnected strategies tend to proliferate in organizations of experts reflecting the complexity of the environments they face and the resulting need for considerable control by the experts over their own work, providing freedom not only from administrators but from their own peers as well. Thus, many hospitals and universities appear to be little more than collections of personal strategies, with hardly any discernible central vision or umbrella, let alone plan, linking them together. Each expert pursues his or her own strategies—method of patient care, subject of research, style of teaching.[5]

This situation may be appropriate for universities and hospitals, but it clearly is not so for business enterprises. What these studies suggest for business is that establishment of a "flexible organization" runs a great risk of making strategy formation worse rather than better. The flexible organization would have to place tremendous reliance on shared visions and values to prevent this from happening. However, as explained in earlier chapters, this reliance would be misplaced.

Flexible Organizations and Organizational Learning

The whole point of flexible structures and dispersed power is to enable those below the top level in the management hierarchy to detect and take action to deal with the large number of changes affecting an organization that operates in a turbulent environment. This is supposed to enable the organization to learn about its environment and so adapt to that environment faster than its rivals do. However, studies have shown that widening participation and empowering people by no means guarantees that organizational learning will improve.[6]

These studies have found that people have a very widespread tendency to approach tasks in group contexts in a manner conditioned by a particular mental model that they apply automatically and unquestioningly. That model consists of certain social values and certain assumptions about effective conduct. Each individual participating in a group normally believes in honesty; in sticking to one's own principles, values, and beliefs; in advocating one's own position and holding that position in the face of others' advocacy; in being rational and thereby avoiding decisions based on emotion; in respecting the feelings of others; and in being caring, helpful, and supportive.

When individuals with these beliefs come together as a group, each assumes that the purpose of the group is as he or she defines it and that if he or she proposes an action, that action should be adopted—in other words, each individual believes in "winning." At the same time, the social values about respect and caring for others lead each individual to conceal criticisms of others' reasoning processes and personal attributes. All individuals in the group make assumptions about the motives of others but never expose those assumptions; praise others wherever possible; tell them whatever will make them feel good without stretching the truth too far; censor themselves under the guise of being caring; and generally try to "save the face" of others as well as of themselves. In short, each individual unilaterally—that is, on his or her own without explicitly consulting the others—tries to control the situation, to win, and yet not hurt others.

However, as each individual tries to implement this behavior, he or she faces a number of dilemmas. That individual can save the face of others only if he or she conceals that this is what is being done. As soon as a "face-saving" device is made public, it loses its efficacy. It therefore becomes necessary to tell "white" lies and to cover up the fact that this is being done. Furthermore, for any one individual to succeed in terms of this model of behavior, all the other members of the group would have to be submissive and dependent. Submissive behavior, however, is not regarded as effective according to the mental model all are using, since that model regards only winning as effective. It follows that one individual can be effective, according to this model, only if he or she makes all the others ineffective. When they use this model, therefore, people get themselves into a double bind: no matter what they do, they cannot win as a group. It is thus not surprising that when a group of people behaving in this way are confronted by embarrassing and uncertain issues, they employ defense routines to avoid having to deal with those issues. They end up playing games, bypassing matters and covering up these bypasses, making matters undiscussable while pretending that they are not doing so, and covering up errors. The result is polarization of issues and widespread deception, with very little real learning.

If we wish to learn new things in highly uncertain situations, we need to approach the learning task from a different perspective. We must come to that task with open, questioning minds rather than an attitude of seeking to win. We have to discuss threatening issues and expose the assumptions we are making about the motives of others so that those assumptions can be publicly tested. If this is not done, we will end up making decisions on the basis of untested information, and that is not a rational thing to do. This approach can be personally risky and threatening, however, so most people avoid doing it. Trying this new mental model takes a great deal of effort, and it is very easy to slip back into the mode in which we conceal things and seek to win rather than to learn.

Since almost everyone uses the mental model that blocks true learning, opening up participation in the learning process to larger numbers of people simply results in many more people performing learning tasks ineffectively. Again, universities provide an example. Participation at most meetings in such institutions is very much more open than it is in businesses, and the win/lose dynamics also are far more prominent. Consequently, while universities may provide excellent conditions for individual learning, the kind of group learning that leads to emergent organizational strategies usually is not much in evidence. If managers wish to improve the ability of an organization to learn, and thus to develop emergent new strategic direction, the first step must be that of tackling ineffective learning models at the individual and small group levels. If participation is widened before this is done, the result is likely to be the spreading of organizational defense routines and game playing, and that will harm rather than help the business.

Flexible structures and dispersed power, then, tend to lead to decision-making processes in which the sequence of choices depends primarily on chance and to the spreading of organizational defense routines and game playing rather than learning. They thus lead to potentially explosive instability (checked only by the extent to which people share a culture and a "vision") rather than either stability or bounded instability.

Boundaries Around Instability

The "flexible organization" model assumes that success is a state of stable consensus. This model relies on strongly shared visions and values to offset the potential instability of equal power, widespread participation, and loose hierarchies. The implicit reasoning behind this model is that top managers can take the chance of loosening structures and empowering people only if they can get those people to share the same approved beliefs, because only then will those people continue, in the absence of rules, to move in the direction determined by the top. In the flexible organization, instead of instructing the army on how to move in detail, the generals rely on their disciplined soldiers to exercise initiative in implementing the grand plan in which they all believe. The importance of strong ideology in flexible organizations is confirmed by the evidence, previously described, that flexible organizations develop into organized anarchies with "garbage-can" decision making and widespread game playing when shared beliefs are weakened. If that weakening of shared beliefs were carried far enough, a flexible organization presumably would disintegrate.

As we have seen in earlier chapters, however, innovative strategies emerge only from the continual challenging of the organizational belief system; that is, from intentional instability. As a consequence, the successful organization's belief system must be weak. If top managers install the other attributes of the flexible organization (equal power, widespread participation, loose hierarchy) and yet keep a weak belief system, they will simply pile instability onto instability. The successful business therefore has to avoid becoming either a conventional "flexible organization," in which stable belief systems destroy innovation, or an organized anarchy, in which organizational strategies rarely emerge. Instead, the successful organization has to occupy the middle ground: a state of chaos, in which instability is intended and encouraged but at the same time is contained within boundaries.

In the dynamic organization, top managers intentionally encourage instability by challenging and provoking people, thereby destroying belief systems. Top managers also intervene in order to affect the boundaries around the consequent instability and the self-organizing processes that produce unpredictable new strategic direction. Two unfamiliar concepts here need further explanation: self-organizing processes and the boundaries around instability.

Consider first what self-organization means for any human system. As soon as a collection of people begin to interact with each other, for example, at a party, we find that particular attitudes, ideas, enthusiasms, propositions, and issues emerge spontaneously within a very short time. People form themselves into groupings around, say, some issue. One group may be for the issue and another against it. Soon the conversation will switch spontaneously to another issue, and the groupings will spontaneously reform. No one directs this process, nor does it move according to a plan: it is a self-organizing process.

This process of spontaneous self-organization is evident in all human systems, including business organizations, if we look for it. In particular, the informal network of contacts between managers in a business is clearly such a self-organizing system. Networks consist of short-lived groupings and regroupings of managers around particular issues, enthusiasms, proposals, or people. Networks are self-camouflaging, invisible, uncountable, and unpollable. No one can make networks happen, design them, or control them. They happen because of the intrinsic property of a human system to self-organize. It was argued in Chapter Four that this self-organizing network system is the strategic control system of a business. Chapter Nine presents some recommendations about intervening to provoke self-organizing processes for this purpose.

Although no one can control an informal network, managers can affect the context within which networks operate or the boundaries around them. These boundaries affect the formation, activity levels, and degree of stability of the networks. At one extreme, managers may tighten the boundaries so much that networks become either relatively inactive and thus stable or active in a covert way and thus unstable. At the other extreme, managers may loosen the boundaries so much that networks become hyperactive and produce organizational anarchy. The best choices of intervention produce states of chaos in which instability is constrained and organizations can function creatively.

Hierarchical structure and the distribution of power provide one boundary around self-organizing processes. Organizational culture provides another. Let us look at each of these boundaries in turn and see how top management can affect them.

Hierarchy and Power

A clear and simple hierarchy of managers, in which power is unequally distributed, jobs are carefully defined, and levels of responsibility and authority accurately established, is required to manage the day-to-day affairs of the business in an effective manner. Such a hierarchy is both possible and appropriate in the conditions of closed and contained change that apply to the short term. This system is also necessary to legitimize the allocation of resources and significant departures from existing activities. Hierarchy and bureaucracy thus are vital for short-term efficiency and stability. Informal networks, on the other hand, exist for exactly the opposite purpose. It is their role to undermine and destroy the hierarchical bureaucracy by bringing to the surface and discussing new issues arising in conditions of open-ended change. The operation of the network system determines the long-term development of the business and the way that the hierarchical bureaucracy changes.

Network operations obviously generate instability. That instability, however, is constrained—first, because it exists in contradiction and tension with the hierarchy, and second, because of its political mode of operation. The manner in which network systems are constrained by the hierarchy is obvious: choices emerging from network operation have to be legitimized, and hierarchical authority confers important advantages to particular players in the network system. A boundary is thus provided by the fact that different people have different levels of power, but none is too powerful. Power is distributed, but it is unequal. A second boundary arises from the fact that power in the network system derives not only from hierarchical authority but also from influence based on others' judgments of one's ability to contribute. Such a system produces sequences of behavior and choice that are constrained by the need to convince, persuade, and maintain political support. This political activity prevents wild swings in behavior and choice unless the boundaries around it are too tight or too loose.

The tightness or looseness of boundaries around a network system is determined by the manner in which managers, especially those at the top, intervene to use their power. Managers must decide when to use their authority (derived from hierarchy), when to rely instead on their influence, and when to refrain from exerting their power at all. If managers apply their authority in all situations, they establish very tight boundaries around the network system. They ensure a system in which people are either submissive or rebellious; as a result, the network either becomes largely dormant or operates covertly. Perhaps surprisingly, charismatic leaders tend to have much the same effect as authoritarian ones. The followers of charismatic leaders are also dependent and submissive, willingly surrendering their critical faculties in the utopian hope that the leader will produce what is required. Such an emotional climate does not encourage the active operation of networks. Even more harmfully, it greatly reduces the need to work at sustaining political support. Under these conditions it becomes all too easy for top managers either to pursue haphazard sequences of decisions or to go off in a single direction to disaster. For the managers' subordinates the boundaries are too tight, but for the managers themselves the boundaries have been removed.

If, instead of using their authority all the time, top managers frequently use only their influence or even make space for those lower down to take the initiative, a different kind of boundary condition or context for the operation of the networks results. Here the boundaries are looser, yet constraint still exists. (The mental models of control managers employ and the way they intervene to use their power will be the subject of two recommendations to be made in the next chapter.)

Another possible set of boundary conditions is produced when structures are flexible and power widely dispersed, as in the flexible organization. We have already seen how this leads to highly unstable sequences of decisions that depend upon chance and widespread defensive behavior. This flexibility, which is essentially an attempt to build the informal network system into a formal reporting structure, has the effect of damaging both the network and the structure.

Organizational Cultures and Learning Capability

Organizational cultures also form a boundary around network operations and thus constrain instability. When managers explore open-ended issues in groups, they are engaging in complex learning. Through this learning they discover how to frame issues and what to do about them. If they all share the same culture, they will all reach much the same conclusions. If this consensus is wrong, as it often will be in a rapidly changing environment, the whole group will pursue a given sequence of decisions for a long time before they realize their error. If, however, they have different cultures, they will approach each issue from different perspectives and frame it in different ways. The conflict that this generates will prevent the group from pursuing one line of reasoning for lengthy periods. This constraint provides a boundary around the instability of learning and decision making. However, it is desirable that some culture be shared. If a group of people trying to learn together share almost nothing in cultural terms, they will do little but conflict.

Both strong sharing and the failure to share culture at all have the effect of creating boundaries that are too tight or too loose; they establish a context that is inappropriate to complex learning. Weakly shared, multiple cultures, on the other hand, both generate instability and provide a boundary around that instability. The boundary is provided by the need to persuade others to follow a line of reasoning.

A group's collective skill at complex learning also provides a boundary around instability. The more effective the people constituting the group are at complex learning, the more they will be able to contain the instability that their learning inevitably generates. This, too, will be the subject of a recommendation in Chapter Nine.

Contradictory Structures and Creative Tension

As this chapter has shown, many management advisors today recommend that managers respond to the complex and rapidly changing business environment by establishing a "flexible organization" characterized by unclear roles, widespread participation in decision making, and relatively equal power distribution. A chief feature of such an organization is a system of self-managing teams held together by strongly shared ideologies, visions, and values.

Unfortunately, this kind of organizational structure tends to destroy the short-interval control system a business must rely on when it handles the predictable. Furthermore, an ideology strong enough to hold the "flexible organization" together establishes the kind of stability that kills innovation, because shared ideology blocks complex learning by demanding a suspension of people's critical faculties. If the ideology is not strong enough, on the other hand, the flexible organization simply disintegrates into organized anarchy. If managers install only some of the trappings of equal participation in an attempt to motivate people, they run the risk of demoralizing those people, who soon perceive the attempt to manipulate.

Adopting a dynamic systems perspective leads to a different response. This perspective recognizes the great importance of hierarchy, unequal power, and clear role definitions in the short-interval control of a business. At the same time, it recognizes the importance of self-organizing political networks in managing the unknowable long term and the necessary constraints on their operation provided by clear hierarchies, unequally distributed power, and countercultures.

Self-organizing networks, an essential feature of dynamic organizations, differ from the flexible organization's self-managing teams in the following important ways:

- Self-organization is a fluid process in which informal, temporary teams form spontaneously around issues, whereas the self-managing teams of the flexible organization are permanent and formally established parts of a reporting structure.

- Top managers cannot control self-organizing networks—they can only intervene to influence the boundary conditions around them—whereas top managers can install a structure of self-managing teams and control them through the rules that govern how the teams are to operate.
- Participants decide who takes part in self-organizing networks and what the boundaries around their activities are, whereas top managers make these decisions with regard to self-managing teams.
- Self-organizing networks operate in conflict with and are constrained by the hierarchy, whereas self-managing teams replace the hierarchy.
- Unequal power energizes self-organizing networks through conflict but also operates as a constraint, whereas dispersed power in self-managing teams is supposed to lead to consensus.
- People in self-organizing networks empower themselves, whereas in self-managing teams, the top empowers people.
- The self-organizing process is both provoked and constrained by cultural difference, whereas the self-managing process is based on strongly shared culture.

The dynamic system perspective recognizes the importance of contradiction and creative tension between the clear-cut, rigid forms of control required to handle the knowable and the self-organizing forms of control required to handle the unknowable, both of which operate simultaneously. These different forms of control call for different forms of behavior alternately by the same people and simultaneously by different people. The choice is not the "either/or" one of the flexible organization perspective but the "both/and" one of the dynamic system perspective.

How are managers to determine whether it is appropriate at any given time to operate in the hierarchical or the network mode? There can be no general answer to that question because it is impossible to apply a general test to every issue to determine whether it is going to have escalating, open-ended, long-term consequences or not. In each situation managers have to use their own judgment and apply the appropriate process. Managers, as skilled professionals, make these choices automatically. As soon as they disagree with hierarchically made decisions they switch to networking, and for this they neither require nor seek permission—the choice is self-organizing.

9

Steps Toward Managing an Unknowable Future

An understanding of recent scientific discoveries about nonlinear feedback systems, which include business organizations, provides a new mental model that can help managers understand their organization's place in today's complex, confusing business world. This model can help managers design actions to cope with that world more realistically than they can do by using the mental model of business success that prevails today. The current mental model focuses on stable equilibrium as the hallmark of success. Once managers understand the new discoveries, however, they will realize that neither stability nor explosive instability but bounded instability, also called chaos, is the true state of a successful business. The constant creativity and innovation necessary for success can occur only in this state.

Managers of any business face a spectrum of changing situations. At one extreme of that spectrum are situations of closed change, in which the short-term consequences of events and actions are predictable. At the other extreme are situations of open-ended change, which especially affect the long-term future of the business. The new understanding of chaos makes clear that the long-term consequences of events and actions affecting nonlinear feedback systems are inherently unpredictable. As a result, it is impossible to have a vision of a business's future state or plan a series of actions that will lead to a specified long-term outcome.

To succeed, managers must control and develop their business during all kinds of change. The forms of control and development they need to use, however, are dictated by the nature of the changes. Applying planning forms of control and development to short-term, predictable change is not only possible but essential. Because the details of the long-term future are completely unknowable, however, managers have to adopt a different form of control and development to deal with long-term or open-ended change. This kind of control relies on processes of self-organizing political interaction and complex learning. Managers who use these processes are not abandoning concern with the long term. They are simply showing a realistic recognition of the ambiguous and uncertain nature of the long-term future.

The need to apply totally different forms of control and development at the same time inevitably creates tension and instability. Successful managers realize that such tension and instability, far from being undesirable, are essential for the creativity that spawns successful business strategy. They therefore deliberately attempt to create conditions of bounded instability. In order to deal with the resulting tension, they become skilled in handling ambiguous issues, revealing contention, and generating new perspectives. They learn how to explore small changes to develop self-reinforcing virtuous circles. They consciously manage the unknowable, relying on the self-organizing processes from which innovative organizational strategies may emerge. Those strategies appear partly as a result of the creative actions of managers themselves; partly as a result of the responses their actions provoke from rivals, customers, suppliers, and regulators; and partly as a result of chance.

It is relatively easy to set out lists of prescriptions to tell managers how to carry out the directing forms of control that should be applied to situations of closed or contained change. It is far more difficult to identify what they should do to apply the enabling forms of control that allow new strategic directions to emerge during open-ended change. That difficulty follows from the very nature of open-ended change—its present ambiguity and future unknowability, the anxiety and conflict it arouses in people. However, there are a number of steps managers can take to increase the likelihood of emergent strategy. These may be grouped under the following seven headings:

- Developing a new understanding of control
- Designing appropriate uses of power
- Establishing self-organizing learning teams
- Developing multiple cultures
- Taking risks
- Improving group learning skills
- Creating resource slack

Each of these ways of enabling emergent strategy is discussed in this chapter.

Developing a New Understanding of Control

Many top management teams are frightened by being told that creative organizationwide strategies cannot be intended or planned ahead of time. Some resist the idea and continue trying to establish prior organizational intention. In doing so they either block the discovery of emergent strategy altogether or restrict participation in the process to a small number of people at the top of the organization. Such restriction may be successful if the people in question possess outstanding business ability and are dealing with a reasonably small organization. These conditions do not apply to most corporations, however.

When top management teams are told that their role is not to set intention but to enable the emergence of strategy by creating the conditions in which key groups of managers can discover new directions, these top managers often respond that limiting themselves to such a role amounts to abdicating control and issuing an open invitation to managers throughout the organization to do whatever they like. These executives feel that if they abandon the setting of overall intention and guiding rules for the long term, one of two consequences will result. Either newly freed lower managers will enthusiastically undertake high volumes of inconsistent and duplicated actions that expose the business to unacceptable levels of risk, or managers exposed to the uncertainty accompanying the absence of clear organizational intention will focus excessively on the short term and avoid strategic thought and action altogether. The top managers believe that they can maintain order and stability only if they establish a consistent framework within which other rungs of management develop specific strategic actions. They never question the assumptions that order and stability are desirable and that lower levels of management are incapable of dealing responsibly with high levels of uncertainty.

This kind of response is evidence of a mental model of control that is out of touch with the realities of open-ended change. Abandoning a view of strategic control as the checking of progress along a predetermined path to a prior intention does not in fact mean abandoning control. It merely means abandoning an inappropriate form of control and replacing it with a more appropriate form. It means abandoning the fantasy of stability in favor of the reality of bounded instability. Establishing the conditions in which managers at different levels can create and discover emergent strategy does not amount to an invitation to people to do whatever they like, provided that there are boundary conditions. Clear hierarchies of managers in which power is by definition unequally distributed provide one important boundary condition. Such hierarchies require that managers build appropriate levels of support before they embark on any new direction. They must use the standard procedures in their organization to get their proposals legitimized and obtain allocation of the resources necessary to carry out their ideas. In other words, the distribution of power and the operation of the political system of the organization will perform control functions even where there is no prior intention or clear direction. A properly functioning political system exerts this control at all levels of the organization. Even a chief executive will have to secure political support in order to carry out particular proposals.

The argument that managers will abandon all concern with the strategic if they are given no clear intention from above is also based on a restrictive mental model of control. The activity of learning in a group is itself a form of control. It is a self-organizing, self-policing kind of control in which the group discovers its own intention and manages itself. Different perspectives and different cultures also provide boundaries around instability. They force managers to look at open-ended issues from many angles and prevent a group from all moving together in disastrous directions.

The first essential step toward creating the conditions under which innovative strategy can emerge is changing the mental model of managers at the top. Without this, inappropriate forms of control will continue. When top managers come to see politics and group learning as forms of control that require no prior organizationwide intention, they will be able to let go. They will come to see that control can be exerted by operating on the boundaries of strategy formation, not the process or the outcome. They will come to see that the benefits of instability are worth the price of a certain amount of inconsistency and duplication.

Designing Appropriate Uses of Power

We are all accustomed to the idea that the strategic direction of communities, nations, and international groups is developed and controlled through the operation of political systems. We describe a system as political when a sequence of choices and actions in that system is produced by the application and exercise of power. The political process is one of identifying issues and building support until it becomes powerful enough to result in the enactment of particular responses to the identified issues. We do not all have to share the same intention, only agree on the same action. A sequence of choices and actions will continue in a particular direction only as long as those espousing that direction continue to enjoy sufficient support. That support is sustained by exercising power either as force of some sort, as authority according to the rules and regulations of the system, or as influence expressed through persuasion and negotiation. Attracting attention for issues, followed by building and sustaining support, occurs largely behind the scenes in informal ways pursued by "men in gray suits" operating in "smoke-filled rooms." Political systems also have more public faces, however, consisting of institutions and procedures by means of which choices and actions are legitimized and given public backing and through which their consequences are accounted for.

Business organizations also have political systems. These systems, like local or national ones, are run by largely informal processes through which issues are identified and support built to attend to them, combined with more public processes that legitimize choices and actions, allocate resources, and account for consequences. The informal aspects of the business political system involve much the same formation of special interest groups, coalitions, factions, and "pressure groups" as do local or national political systems. It is here that the real political power is applied, the real support sustained, and the real choices made. Similarly, the public aspects of the business political system include formal bodies, such as the board of directors, that legitimize the choices made more informally and account for the financial consequences of the enactment of those choices.

Curiously, however, although most managers would immediately describe the political process when asked how nations develop and control policy, few do so when asked how companies develop and control strategic direction. Managers seem to dislike thinking of themselves as politicians, and most seem to shy away from explicit examination of how they and their colleagues use power. On the surface, this attitude toward politics may be explained by the negative connotations of politics for many: lying, cheating, manipulating, and self-seeking. More careful reflection, however, reveals that not all politics is like this—there are fundamental political processes that are used for getting things done. At a deeper level, business people may avoid explicit examination of business politics because it conflicts with their belief that strategy should be intentionally set ahead of time through a rational process and controlled directly by monitoring outcomes against predetermined targets. The discovery of the applicability of chaos to business systems requires managers to question this mental model. Chaos points to a model in which strategic direction emerges from a political process through which individual intentions may converge. Organizational intention thus becomes retrospective rather than prospective, a consequence of the way power was exerted.

As soon as we see strategic direction as the consequence of choices that emerge from a political process, we have to pay explicit attention to the way we apply power. Effective strategic management depends upon how managers design their use of power. This is true because the manner in which power is used has a direct impact on the dynamics of group interaction, and group dynamics in turn have a powerful effect on the way managers in that group work together and what they learn. What they learn together determines the strategic choices they make and the actions they take. The distribution of power and the way in which it is used provide very important boundaries around the group learning process from which new strategic directions emerge. By managing those boundaries, top managers exert control. To be sure, they do not control the learning process itself, the sequences of choices made, or the outcomes of those choices. Such control is impossible when the dynamic is chaotic. Instead, their control takes an enabling form. By managing boundary conditions to produce bounded instability, top managers make it possible for real learning to occur and new strategic directions to emerge.

Applying Power

The application of power in particular forms has fairly predictable consequences for broad categories of group dynamics. When power is applied as force and consented to out of fear, the group dynamics will focus on submission. When power applied in this way is not consented to, the group dynamics will focus on rebellion, either covert or overt. If an organization faces a clear threat, the use of power as force may well produce the required results. But where the organization faces an ambiguous, open-ended future, the application of force is disastrous. Groups in states of either submission or rebellion are incapable of the complex learning that results in the development of new perspectives, new mental models, and innovative strategic directions. All the energy of such groups will go into avoidance or fighting.

Power is applied as authority when that application is in accordance with the procedures and rules of the organization and is consented to on that basis. In the predictable group dynamics here, members of the group suspend their critical faculties and accept instructions from those above them. The dynamics focus on dependence and conformity. This is an appropriate use of power and a beneficial group state when an organization faces closed and contained change. Under these circumstances, intention can be agreed upon and incorporated into rules and procedures. Dependence upon and conformity with the instructions of authority will produce efficient behavior. This is the form of power and the group dynamics required for short-interval control. But when the situation is open ended, this application of power and the dynamics it provokes are disastrous. Conforming groups in which individuals have suspended their critical faculties, like submissive or rebellious groups, are incapable of complex learning and creative strategy formation.

In the group dynamics conducive to complex learning, highly competitive win/lose polarization is absent. The dynamics focus on open questioning and public testing of views and assertions. People use argument and conflict around issues to move toward periodic consensus and commitment concerning a particular issue, yet consensus and commitment are not the norm. They cannot be if people are searching for new perspectives all the time. A group successfully engaged in complex learning is not dominated by dependence on authority or expert figures. Its members neither avoid issues nor seek unilaterally to control them. The group alternates between conflict and consensus, between confusion and clarity. Its dynamics have the characteristics of chaos. The principal boundaries around the group's instability are provided by the manner in which the most powerful use their power and the existence of countercultures.

The application of power most consistent with the kind of group dynamics required to enable complex learning is likely to be a variable one. The most powerful group members will sometimes withdraw and allow conflict, sometimes intervene with suggestions and influence, and sometimes impose authority or even force. When managers use power in this variable way they sustain the instability required to provoke new perspectives. That instability nonetheless is bounded because authority, clear hierarchy, and unequally distributed power still exist. No recipe can determine the best use of power in specific circumstances. The true skill of the enabling leader lies in the ability to design the best use of power in each situation, based on experience, reflection, and judgment.

Distributing Power

If power is highly concentrated and is always applied as force or authority, the result is a very stable organization in which little complex learning occurs because the boundary conditions are too tight. The organization can then deal only with whatever open-ended change the most powerful notice and are capable of handling. Strategy becomes the result of the intention of the top executive, and unless that executive is exceptionally talented, the organization will fail to develop sufficiently creative new strategic directions to survive.

If power is widely distributed and hardly ever used as authority, on the other hand, the result is organized anarchy. Again, very little complex learning occurs, this time because the boundary conditions are too loose. Instead of new strategic direction for the organization as a whole, we find fragmented strategies arising from individual intentions that rarely converge because the group dynamics encourage only continual conflict or avoidance.

If power is unequal but distributed and applied in forms that alternate according to the circumstances, we find a flexible, fluctuating boundary around the political process that enables complex learning. It is important to note, however, that establishing such a boundary does not ensure that complex learning will occur or that it will produce some outcome that can be predetermined or guaranteed to be successful. The political and learning activity that may produce creative choices is spontaneous and self-organizing. We cannot instruct anyone to have a creative idea in an open-ended situation. We cannot orchestrate factions and coalitions between people that will be guaranteed to support the right idea, because when the situation is open ended we cannot know what the right idea is. All we can do is set up the boundaries within which behavior favorable to the emergence of an innovative choice might occur.

Establishing Self-organizing Learning Teams

The heart of strategic management is a flexible, ever-changing agenda of open-ended issues that is identified, clarified, and progressed by the self-organizing networks of an organization. Top managers cannot install or take control of such a network system. But they can create the atmosphere in which it operates effectively and they can intervene to increase network activity levels. For example, top management can set up teams of key managers to explore parts or all of the strategic agenda. Workshops and multidisciplinary task forces are examples of such teams.

These learning teams must operate in a spontaneous and self-organizing manner if they are to be effective. Self-organization here does not mean formal or informal participation by representatives of the entire organization. It is not, as was made clear in Chapter Eight, the same thing as self-managing teams. Self-organization is based on people's judgments of each other's potential contributions. It is political interaction carried out within the boundaries of unequal power and hierarchy. It is complex learning carried out within the boundaries of different personalities and cultures.

Designing the Teams

A self-organizing group of the sort being described here is not just any group of people thrown together. Such a group has a design. That design flows from self-selection, in which individuals select other individuals either on the basis of expected contribution or in order to form a faction or coalition related to some issue. When this self-designing process is operating at a very low level of activity, it may be possible for top managers to encourage it—to kick start it—by formally selecting subordinates to form a group. Such subordinates should be chosen on the basis of personality and likely contribution, not position in the formal hierarchy. The effectiveness of learning groups may be increased by tying performance appraisal to contribution to the groups.

Since the purpose of setting up these self-organizing teams is to generate new perspectives, it is important to draw the teams' membership from a number of different functions, business units, and hierarchical levels. Doing this also helps to overcome the inherent inflexibility of existing structures and systems. In particular, middle management in most companies is a resource much underutilized for developing new strategic directions. Middle managers are closer to the action of the marketplace than those higher up and thus are more likely to detect the sort of contradictions, anomalies, and changes from which new strategic directions may emerge.

Presenting Challenges

Different learning teams can have different focuses. One team may work on strategy for the organization as a whole. This group should not simply replicate the board or other formal top executive team, however; it should involve other levels of the organization as well. Strategy groups also may be formed for a particular business unit or function, but they should include people from other units and functions too. Task forces may be set up to develop specific projects.

A team can be truly self-organizing only if it discovers its own goals and objectives. This means that top managers setting up such a team must avoid the temptation to write terms of reference, set objectives, or prod the group to reach some predetermined conclusion. They must limit themselves to presenting the group with some ambiguous challenge. For example, they might challenge a group to produce proposals for a new product or promotional campaign. Alternatively, the challenge may be more general, such as finding a better organizational structure or simply identifying strategic issues by looking for contradictions and anomalies in the marketplace. Challenges should be deliberately chosen to provoke the kind of emotion and conflict that can lead to an active search for new ways of doing things.

This activity of presenting challenges should be a two-way process: top executives should hold themselves open to challenge from subordinates as well as vice versa. General Electric has developed such two-way challenges into a regular process that it calls the "workout." During a workout, a manager talks to his or her team and outlines his or her views on how they should operate. The team members discuss the ideas and issues among themselves. They then reconvene with their manager to discuss the issues. This manager can accept the ideas for improvement presented in the discussion, reject them, or promise to think further about them. If such a promise is made, the manager must report back to the team with a final decision within thirty days.

The workout process is applied rigorously across the hierarchy from top to bottom. It is structured so that managers cannot get away with doing nothing. Independent experts act as facilitators. They sit in on the sessions, make sure that managers do not bully those who speak their minds, and check to see that the managers keep their promises. The aim is to create an atmosphere in which speaking out and telling the truth are not only acceptable but rewarded.

Teams of managers can be self-organizing only if they are free to operate as their members jointly choose, within the boundaries provided by their work together. This means that the normal hierarchy must be suspended most of the time during such a group's work. The higher-level members of the group must indicate by their behavior that they attach little importance to their position while they are in the group. They should show clear recognition that all group members are present because of the contributions they can make and the influence they can exert through their contributions and personalities. Note that these groups do not replace or weaken the hierarchy. They are temporary occasions in which managers use their power in a different way. Outside the meeting they will revert again to normal authority.

Top managers must give these self-organizing learning groups their formal interest and support regardless of what the groups produce. There is no point in setting up such groups unless those at the top are genuinely looking for a new perspective. Top executives must be willing to take the chance that the groups will produce proposals of which they do not approve—or even no proposals at all. Support from the top must include permission to fail.

It must be stressed that establishing workshops and meetings of the kind described here is not meant to become a permanent part of the structure. Setting these groups up is simply an intervention that tries to send messages about and prompt greater levels of spontaneous self-organizing behavior.

Developing Multiple Cultures

New perspectives seldom appear when people strongly share the same culture and therefore use the same unconscious mental models to interpret what is going on around them and to design their responses to change. Managers usually see their organizational challenge as one of bringing about a common culture, but in fact it is far more difficult to keep different cultures alive because of the power of group conformity. Top management therefore should actively promote countercultures in the organization.

Management can encourage countercultures in a number of ways. The first is to rotate people between functions and business units. Doing this is usually seen merely as a way of giving executives wider experience within the same business philosophy. This tendency to build up a cadre of managers with the same philosophy needs to be overcome by designing development programs that stress the importance of cultural diversity rather than uniformity.

An even more effective way of promoting countercultures is practiced by Canon and Honda, who hire managers in significant numbers midway through their careers in other organizations. They do this for the express purpose of establishing sizable pockets of new cultures that conflict with the predominant culture. It is important that this should be done at different levels in the hierarchy, not merely confined to one or two top executives.

A third possibility is to use outsiders on some of the self-organizing teams in the organization. Outsiders can be people from another function or business unit within the company or, probably to greater effect, they may be people from outside the company and the industry, for example, management consultants.

Taking Risks

Top managers in large organizations face a choice. First, they can choose to take a chance and enable the unpredictable emergence of new strategies. The process will be accompanied by conflict, disorder, and inconsistency. A strategy may emerge or it may not. It may be a successful strategy or it may not.

The other choice is to try to reduce risk by applying directing forms of control in all situations, including those of open-ended change. Managers who follow this path insist that everyone in their company adhere to the same long-term vision, values, or plan. Alternatively, they recommend that the company stick to the business it knows best and avoid long-term investments. In effect they say, "Either find a way to control the outcome of your actions or don't do anything." The end of this path is the predictable blocking of the emergence of new strategic directions and usually failure to achieve the vision or plan as well. At best, the organization will be temporarily successful before succumbing to more imaginative rivals.

What seems like the safer alternative thus turns out to be the more dangerous one, because it does not take into account the dynamics of the business game. Trying to control the outcome of open-ended situations carries with it the certainty of ultimate failure, whereas trying to enable the emergence of new strategic directions offers at least the possibility of success. In business there is no sensible alternative to taking chances.

Managers who wish to develop creatively have to remain open to the possibility of the "revolution," the radical departure from the existing business. For example, NEC's main business originally was the delivery of products and components made to the special specifications of Nippon Telegraph and Telephone Company. Nonaka describes how that business changed:

> The new product development process began when a group from the Semiconductor and IC Sales Division conceived of an idea to sell Japan's first microcomputer kit, the TK-80, to promote the sales of semiconductor devices. Selling the TK-80 to the public at large was a radical departure from NEC's history of filling NTTP's routine orders. Unexpectedly, a wide variety of customers, ranging from high school students to professional computer enthusiasts, came to NEC's "BIT-INN," a display service center in Akihabara. The continuing dialogues with these customers at "BIT-INN" resulted in the eventual best-selling personal computer PC-8000.[1]

In his study of international companies, Michael Porter concludes that the companies that build sustainable competitive advantage on a global scale are the ones that intentionally set out to serve the world's most sophisticated and demanding customers and compete with the most imaginative and competent rivals. They make long-term investments in training and development, research, and infrastructure without having any guarantee of specific returns. They also encourage the development of clusters of effective suppliers.[2] Thus, far from trying to avoid risk, managers who understand the inherently complex and risky nature of the business climate and the unpredictability of the long-term future recognize the need to seek out challenges in order to continue to develop competitive advantage.

Improving Group Learning Skills

New strategic directions emerge when groups of managers learn together in a complex way. Their learning is complex because it is not simply the absorption of existing bodies of knowledge, sets of techniques, or recipes and prescriptions. It is the alteration of existing mental models of how things work, how people perceive what is going on, and how they learn together and interact with each other. It is the development of new models with which to interpret new situations. It involves continual questioning of deeply held and usually unconscious beliefs. Finally, this learning is complex because it can be threatening; it arouses anxiety and thus possibly bizarre group dynamics.

Given this complexity, group learning skills cannot be improved by taking neatly packaged courses. Each group must seek its own ways to improve learning skills. This task means bringing to the surface and discussing the assumptions people are making. It means revealing and dealing with defense mechanisms, game playing, and other behavior that blocks learning. Even top managers must participate in this process; indeed, they need to enable it and create the context of openness that it demands.

Because the examination and improvement of learning skills is so important, meetings or workshops devoted to this task need to be ongoing and frequent. Often they are best done with some form of outside facilitation. Personality tests may be helpful here, provided that they are used not in a mechanistic way but as a means of giving insight into why certain behavior is occurring. In his book *The Fifth Discipline,* Peter Senge describes the program installed by the insurance company Hanover.[3] This program was a continuing, long-term effort in which managers could work on their learning models and expose their defensive routines. Perhaps as a result of the program, Hanover has consistently outperformed the industry averages for profitability.

Creating Resource Slack

The creative work needed to deal with open-ended issues takes time and management resources, and investment in this activity has an unpredictable return. For lengthy periods it is quite possible that little will emerge from a great deal of discussion and experimentation. But without this investment in what appears to be management resource slack, new strategic directions will not emerge. A vital precondition for emergent strategy is thus enough investment in management resources to allow it to happen. This runs counter to requirements for short-term profit and efficiency, but it is a price that must be paid if new strategic directions are to emerge. The current fashion for cutting out layers of middle management, for reducing numbers of senior executives and loading them up with day-to-day duties, can easily be taken so far that it destroys the ability of a company to attend to open-ended issues. Executives who work twelve or fourteen hours a day are unlikely to have the mental resources to attend to such issues. A careful judgment therefore has to be made concerning the amount of management resource slack required to enable emergent strategy.

Applying Different Control Forms Simultaneously

As mentioned at the beginning of this chapter, the control forms necessary to foster emergent strategy must coexist with the very different forms of control that are appropriate to handling short-term situations involving closed or contained change. A business also has to practice short-interval control through negative feedback applied by means of formal structures, systems, and plans. Such day-to-day control should be based on clear organizational intention and secured through setting quantitative, time-specific objectives. It requires clear hierarchies and organizational structures with precise job definitions. Since organizational structures are largely irrelevant to the emergence of new strategic direction, these structures should be designed to yield the most effective short-interval control and to deliver competitive advantage to known market segments. The same applies to formal information and control systems. Organizational structures and formal information and control systems should be changed only when an emerged strategy makes this necessary.

At the same time a business is applying this very structured kind of control to the short term, it must use amplifying feedback to create the bounded instability necessary for handling open-ended issues and enabling strategy to emerge from political action and complex learning. Control in these circumstances means operating on the boundary conditions around necessary instability rather than establishing organizational intention. It means provoking conflict around issues, encouraging divergent cultures, and presenting ambiguous challenges.

The need to use both of these forms of control simultaneously means that a significant number of key managers must be capable of alternating the ways they work and behave. At some times they have to rely on analysis and the application of authority in formal situations, while at other times they must rely on their own personalities and influence in informal political settings. They have to use analogous reasoning and intuitive abilities. They have to challenge and be open to challenge. Above all, they have to develop the ability to learn with others in complex, sometimes threatening ways.

The key message of the dynamic systems model is that a preoccupation with order, stability, and consistency in all time frames damages management's creativity and ability to cope with the unknowable. When the future is unknowable, managers cannot install techniques, procedures, structures, and ideologies to control long-term outcomes. They can, however, manage boundary conditions in a way that pushes the organization into the area far from equilibrium in which spontaneous self-organization may occur and new strategic directions may emerge. The key question managers face, then, is not how to maintain stable equilibrium but how to establish sufficient constrained instability to provoke complex learning. It is through political interaction and complex learning that businesses create and manage their unknowable futures.

NOTES

Chapter One

1. Hampden-Turner, C. *Charting the Corporate Mind: From Dilemma to Strategy*. Oxford: Blackwell, 1990.
2. De Geus, P. "Planning as Learning." *Harvard Business Review*, March-April 1988, 70-74.
3. Peters, T. J., and Waterman, R. H. *In Search of Excellence*. New York: HarperCollins, 1982.
4. Pascale, R. T. *Managing on the Edge: How Successful Companies Use Conflict to Stay Ahead*. London: Viking Penguin, 1990.
   Miller, D. *The Icarus Paradox: How Excellent Organizations Can Bring About Their Own Downfall*. New York: Harper Business, 1990.
   Hamel, G., and Prahalad, C. K. "Strategic Intent." *Harvard Business Review*, May-June 1989, 63-76.
5. Miller, *The Icarus Paradox*.
6. Senge, P. *The Fifth Discipline*. New York: Doubleday, 1990.
7. For more information on how system dynamics applies to nature's systems and about the mathematics involved, see:
   Gleick, J. *Chaos: Making a New Science*. Portsmouth, N.H.: Heineman, 1987.
   Stewart, I. *Does God Play Dice? The Mathematics of Chaos*. Oxford: Blackwell, 1989.

8. For more information on how the theories of management can be related to modern scientific theories of complex dynamics, see:
Stacey, R. D. *The Chaos Frontier: Creative Strategic Control for Business.* Oxford: Butterworth-Heinemann, 1991.
9. Nonaka, I. "Creating Organizational Order out of Chaos: Self-Renewal in Japanese Firms." *California Management Review,* Spring 1988, 57–73.

Chapter Two

1. "The Revenge of Big Yellow." *The Economist,* November 1990.
2. Bowman, C., and Asch, D. *Strategic Management.* London: Macmillan, 1987.
3. Greenley, G. T. "Does Strategic Planning Improve Company Performance?" *Long Range Planning,* 1986, *19*(2), 101–109.
4. Goold, M., with Quinn, J. J. *Strategic Control: Milestones for Long Term Performance.* London: Hutchison, 1990.
5. A London Business School Survey, reported in the *Financial Times* (7 November 1990), showed that two-thirds of companies used payback methods.
6. Marsh, P. *Short Termism on Trial.* London: Institutional Fund Managers Association, 1990.
7. Hamel and Prahalad, "Strategic Intent" (see Chapter One, Note 4).
8. Senge, *The Fifth Discipline* (see Chapter One, Note 6).
9. Forrester, J. *Industrial Dynamics.* Cambridge, Mass.: MIT Press, 1961.
10. Senge, *The Fifth Discipline,* p. 73 (see Chapter One, Note 6).
11. Miller, *The Icarus Paradox,* p. 1 (see Chapter One, Note 4).
12. Pascale, *Managing at the Edge* (see Chapter One, Note 4).
13. Schumpeter, J. A. *The Theory of Economic Development.* Cambridge, Mass.: Harvard University Press, 1934.

Chapter Three

1. Peters and Waterman, *In Search of Excellence* (see Chapter One, Note 3).

2.   The Mandelbrot set is named after its discoverer, Benoit
      Mandelbrot. For further information on Mandelbrot sets, see
      the works of Gleick and Stewart (see Chapter One, Note 7).

3.   For the sake of simplicity, the patterns shown for the Mandel-
      brot set have been described in terms of a distinction between
      stability and instability. It is more accurate to describe these
      patterns as a contour map showing the strength of pull to
      instability or infinity. The simplification does not affect the
      points made.

4.   For pictures of the Mandelbrot set in color, see Peitgen, H. O.,
      and Richter, P. H. *The Beauty of Fractals: Images of Complex
      Dynamical Systems*. Heidelberg: Springer-Verlag, 1986.

5.   Gleick, *Chaos: Making a New Science* (see Chapter One,
      Note 7).

6.   Shenkman, J., and Le Baron, B. "Nonlinear Dynamics and
      Stock Returns." *Journal of Business*, 1989, *62*(3).
      Hsieh, D. "Testing for Nonlinear Dependence in Daily For-
      eign Exchange Returns." *Journal of Business*, 1989, *62*(3).
      Peters, P. E. *Chaos and Order in the Capital Markets*. New
      York: Wiley, 1991.

7.   Porter, M. *The Competitive Advantage of Nations*. London:
      Macmillan, 1990.

8.   Arthur, W. B. "Self-Reinforcing Mechanisms in Economics."
      In P. W. Anderson, K. J. Arrow, and D. Pines (eds.), *The
      Economy as a Complex Evolving System*. Reading, Mass.:
      Addison-Wesley, 1988.

9.   Lawrence, P. R., and Lorsch, J. M. *Organization and Environ-
      ment*. Cambridge, Mass.: Harvard University Press, 1967.

Chapter Four

1.   Schumpeter, J. A. *The Theory of Economic Development* (see
      Chapter Two, Note 13).

2.   Prigogine, I., and Stengers, I. *Order out of Chaos: Man's New
      Dialogue with Nature*. London: Heinemann, 1984.

3.   Davies, P. *The Cosmic Blueprint*. London: Heinemann, 1987.

4.   Nonaka, I. "Creating Organizational Order out of Chaos: Self-
      Renewal in Japanese Firms" (see Chapter One, Note 9).

5. Pettigrew, A. M. *The Politics of Organizational Decision Making*. London: Tavistock, 1973.
Pfeffer, J. *Power in Organizations*. Cambridge, Mass.: Bakkinger, 1981.
Kanter, R. M. *The Change Masters: Innovation in the American Corporation*. Englewood Cliffs, N.J.: Simon & Shuster, 1985.
6. Thomas, D. *Alan Sugar: The Amstrad Story*. London: Century, 1990, p. 251.

Chapter Five

1. Baddeley, A. *Human Memory, Theory and Practice*. Hillsdale, N.J.: Erlbaum, 1990.
2. Argyris, C. *Overcoming Organizational Defenses: Facilitating Organizational Learning*. Needham Heights, Mass.: Allyn & Bacon, 1990.
3. Baddeley, *Human Memory*.
4. Gick, M. L., and Holyoak, K. J. "Schema Introduction and Analogical Transfer." *Cognitive Psychology*, 1983, *15*, 1–38.
5. Dawkins, R. *The Blind Watchmaker*. London: Penguin, 1988, p. 198.
6. Goold, M., and Campbell, A. *Strategies and Styles*. Oxford: Blackwell, 1988.
7. Sioshansi, F. *Pricing and Marketing Electricity*. London: The Economist Intelligence Unit, 1990.
8. Senge, P. *The Fifth Discipline* (see Chapter One, Note 6).
9. Argyris, C. *Overcoming Organizational Defenses*.
10. Schein, E. H. *Organizational Culture and Leadership*. San Francisco: Jossey-Bass, 1985.
11. Bion, W. *Experiences in Groups and Other Papers*. London: Tavistock Publications, 1961.
12. Argyris, C. *Overcoming Organizational Defenses*.
13. Bion, *Experiences in Groups*.

Chapter Six

1. Peters, T. *Thriving on Chaos*. London: Macmillan, 1985.

2. Hayek, F. A. von. "Scientism and the Study of Society." *Economica,* 1942, 1943, 1944.

3. Weick, K. *The Social Psychology of Organizing.* Reading, Mass.: Addison-Wesley, 1979.

4. Ries, A., and Trout, J. *Bottom-Up Marketing.* New York: McGraw-Hill, 1989.

5. Miller, D., and Friesen, P. H. "Momentum and Revolution in Organizational Adaptation." *Academy of Management Journal,* 1980, *23,* 591–614.

6. Quinn, J. B. "Strategic Change: 'Logical Incrementalism.'" *Sloan Management Review,* 1978, *20,* 7–21.

7. Mintzberg, H., and Waters, J. A. "Of Strategies Deliberate and Emergent." *Strategic Management Journal,* 1985, *6,* 257–272.

8. Peters, T. *Thriving on Chaos.*

9. Quinn, J. B. "Federal Express Corporation." In J. B. Quinn, H. Mintzberg, and R. M. James (eds.), *The Strategy Process.* Englewood Cliffs, N.J.: Prentice-Hall, 1988.

10. Thomas, *Alan Sugar: The Amstrad Story* (see Chapter Four, Note 6).

11. Campbell, A., and Tawady, K. *Mission and Business Philosophy: Winning Employee Commitment.* London: Heinemann, 1990.

12. Campbell and Tawady, *Mission and Business Philosophy.* Senge, *The Fifth Discipline* (see Chapter One, Note 6).

Chapter Seven

1. Peters, *Thriving on Chaos* (see Chapter Six, Note 1).

2. Ashby, W. R. *Introduction to Cybernetics.* New York: Wiley, 1956.

Chapter Eight

1. Peters, *Thriving on Chaos* (see Chapter Six, Note 1).

2. Kanter, *The Change Masters* (see Chapter Four, Note 5).

3. Kanter, *The Change Masters* (see Chapter Four, Note 5).

4. Cohen, M. D., March, J. G., and Ohlsen, J. P. "A Garbage Can Model of Organizational Choice." *Administrative Science Quarterly,* 1972, *17,* 1–25.

5. Mintzberg and Waters, "Of Strategies Deliberate and Emergent" (see Chapter Six, Note 7).
6. Argyris, *Overcoming Organizational Defenses* (see Chapter Five, Note 2).

Chapter Nine

1. Nonaka, "Creating Organizational Order" (see Chapter Four, Note 4).
2. Porter, M. *The Competitive Advantage of Nations.* London: Macmillan, 1990.
3. Senge, *The Fifth Discipline* (see Chapter One, Note 6).

INDEX

211

Teams
Review
Process
- learned from each other
- Reviews based on ideas
  produced + developed
- New things learned
- contributions to division
- New directions taken w
  clients
- Work shared with each other

Mtg with 2 teams — monthly
to discuss above + observations
• Actions to be taken.
• New ideas

Basic Structure —

  ⎧ 2 Design Teams Promo
  ⎨ 2 Design Teams Catalog
  ⎩ 1 support team
All support each other

Nothing else assumed
Objectives:
  - cross train
  - stimulate new ideas

and projects
- increase productivity
- decrease cost
— more creativity in other
    Div.

Objectives: look at new writers + designers
    — advertising support
    — multi media projects
    — Special projects -
    Cross divisional
    — cross work w Bob + DeSoto
    — support of Hdqtrs work

[ORGANIZED CHAOS]

— bonus program -
set up photo permissions
of WWF files
— Production Schedule computerized